Library of
Davidson College

A Garland Series

British Philosophers and Theologians of the 17th & 18th Centuries

A Collection of 101 Volumes

Edited by
René Wellek

Richard Burthogge

AN ESSAY
UPON
REASON
AND THE
NATURE OF SPIRITS
1694

Garland Publishing, Inc., New York & London

1976

Bibliographical note:

this facsimile has been made from a copy in the
Beinecke Library of Yale University
(Mhc9.B952.E6)

Library of Congress Cataloging in Publication Data

Burthogge, Richard, 1638?-ca. 1700.
    An essay upon reason, and the nature of spirits.

    (British philosophers and theologians of the 17th &
18th centuries ; no. 10)
    Reprint of the 1694 ed. printed for J. Dunton, London.
    1. Knowledge, Theory of. 2. Supernatural. I. Ti-
tle. II. Series.
B1201.B73E6 1976   121   75-11204
ISBN 0-8240-1759-5

Printed in the United States of America

AN
ESSAY
UPON
REASON,
AND THE
Nature of Spirits.

By *Richard Burthogge*, M. D.

LONDON:

Printed for John Dunton at the *Raven* in the *Poultrey*. 1694.

To the Learned

Mr. JOHN LOCK,

Author of the

ESSAY

Upon

Humane Underſtanding.

SIR,

I Take the Liberty of making a Preſent of the following Eſſay unto you, as to a Perſon who being ac-

The Preface.

knowledged by all the **Learned World** *for one of the Greatest Masters of* **Reason**, *are therewithal allowed a most Proper and Competent Judge of any Discourse concerning it. Whatever my Performance is, the* **Design** *I have is no small one; since it is to show the true way of Humane Knowledge, and by shewing that it is* REAL NOTIONAL, *to unite and reconcile the* **Experimental**, *or* **Mechanical**, *with the* **Scholastical Method**. *This Thought, Sir, affords me abundant matter of enlarging in many others; but I ought to remember, that I am*

a

The Preface.

a stranger to you, and this my First Visit, and therefore I must make it short, which I will do, by hastning to own my self among the Croud *of those who do admire you, and to assure you, that I am with great Respect,*

SIR,

Your very Humble Servant

RICH. BURTHOGGE.

ERRA-

ERRATA.

Page 6. Line 3. for *Toubing*, r. *Touching*. p. 10. l. 25. for *preception*, r. *perception*. p. 25. l. 14. *for*, r. *or else*. p. 33. l. 25. for *do*, r. *doth*. p. 42. l. 22. for *diffusiovum*, r. *diffusivum*. Ibid. l. 28. for *est*, r. *&*. p. 52. l. 9. for *spect*, r. *respect*. p. 57. l. 7. for *or*, r. *of*. Ibid. l. 15. dele *time*. Ibid. l. 17. for *Appre*, r. *Apprehends*. p. 60. l. 24. r. *conceptions ut art*. p. 62. l. 24. dele *the*. p. 74. l. 18. for *word*, r. *world*. p. 77. l: 21: dele *not*.

Of Human Reason.

The First Part.

Chap. I. *Of Reason in general.*

SECT. I.

In what sense Reason is taken and discoursed of here. A double account of it; the first, more Notional; the second, more Real. Of the Agreements of Reason, Sense, and Imagination. (1.) That all three are Cogitative and Conceptive Powers. Cogitation what. Monsieur des Cartes, *and* Honoratus Faber, *their Opinion, that Sensation is not Cogitation, considered, (2.) That Sense, Imagination, and Reason are Mental and Spiritual, and not meerly Mechanick and Material Powers. The Differences of those Powers; that all Sensation is Imagination, and what is commonly called Imagination, is but Internal Sensation. Intellection or Reasoning, is Knowing without Imagination. Instances, setting out these several Notions. The power of Knowing without Imagining, why called Reason.*

REASON taken for Human *Mind*, or Understanding (which is the sense I take it in now) is defined by most, the faculty whereby a Man is said to be Reasonable, or Understanding; in like manner as *Sight* is defined, the faculty whereby a Living Creature is Denominated Seeing, or Visive, or Reason is that faculty whereby a Man does Exercise the acts of Reason, or doth Understand; as Sight, the faculty whereby a Man or any other Animal doth see, or discern Objects.

Nor are they altogether without Reason, who do so define and explicate it; for *Acts* of Perception properly so called, are not Known, or Knowable, but in and by themselves; we Know not, nor are capable of Knowing, what the Act of Seeing is, but by seeing; nor what that of Hearing is, but by Hearing; or what the Act of Understanding is, but by Understanding. And again, *Perceptive faculties* are not Known, or Knowable, but by their Acts: We Know not what the faculty or power of Seeing is but *relatively*, with relation to the Act of Seeing: Nor what the faculty or Power of Hearing is, but by the Act of Hearing; nor what the faculty or power of Understanding or Reasoning is, but by *Acts* of Understanding or Reasoning foning: In a word, no Faculties, no Powers are Known, or Knowable, but by their respective Acts or Exercises, and therefore they cannot be defined or set out but by them. All this is certain.

However, since this is but a notional fruitless way of Explicating Reason, and too short, too narrow to satisfie a Curious and Inquisitive Mind; therefore to settle an *Idea* of it, that may be more to purpose, more real, and more edifying; I will show, in the first place, the *Agreements* it hath with other Conceptive Cogitative faculties, what it holds in common with them; and afterwards, set out the *Differences* that do discriminate and divide these several faculties, each from other, and this particularly from the Rest.

The *Conceptive Cogitative* Faculties that are in Man, (for so I call the Faculties by which he makes acquaintance with external Objects) are his external *Sense*, *Imagination* (as it is called) and *Reason* or Understanding: *Three* Faculties which do all *Agree* and Concur in this, that they are *Conceptive* and *Cogitative*, and consequently *Mental* and *Spiritual*, and not meerly *Mechanick* and *Material* Powers.

First; All three are *Conceptive*, *Cogitative* Powers; Sensation and Imagination, as well as Reasoning or Intellection, are

Cogitations.

Cogitations. Cogitation is conscious Affection; *Conscious Affection*, is Affection with Consciousness of that Affection; and by another name is called *Knowledge*. Knowledge, as it has a double relation, so it may be considered two ways, to wit, either in reference to the *Object*, which is Known, and so, properly, it is *Apprehension* or Conscious Perception; or, as it respects the *Image* and *Idea*, by means of which we do perceive or know that Object, and so it may be called *Conception*. Conception properly speaking, is of the Image, or Idea; Apprehension, Knowledge, or conscious Perception is of the Object, by means of that Idea, or Image: It is as proper to say, that the Sense and Imagination do conceive, as that the Reason or Understanding doth; the former does as much conceive Images and Sentiments, as the latter does Ideas and Notions.

Conception and Cogitation, really are but one Act, and consequently, all Conceptive are Cogitative Powers, and Cogitative Powers Conceptive. Only, to clear the Notion of *Consciousness*, by which *Cogitation* or Knowledge is distinguished, tho' never divided, from *Conception*, we must further consider the *Way* and Manner how Consciousness Arises. And it seems to me to *arise*, ordinarily, from the distinction and

and difference that is in Conceptions; for, should any person have his Eye perpetually tied to one Object, without ever closing of, or turning it to another, he would no more be sensible that he *saw* that Object, or know any more what it was to *see*, than if he had been blind from his Birth. For since *Consciousness of Seeing* is nothing but a perceiving by the Eye, that one is Affected, or otherwise Affected than he was, with the appearance of Light, or Colour. If a person had never seen but one thing, and never but seen it, he could have no perceivance (that) he is so Affected, that is, he could not be sensible or conscious (that) he did see. Thus, tho' in our Members the parts that do compose them are contiguous one to another, and do always touch, yet we do not feel them touch, that is, they touch, but we are not sensible they do, because no difference being in the Affection, there is no Sense, no Consciousness of it: But Dislocation is soon perceived; as also it is when any part is pressed unusually. I conclude, that as difference of Conception arises from different Affections of the Faculties by Objects, so Consciousness, or Sense of Conception, arises from the difference of Conceptions. Did we know but one thing, or had but one Act of Conception, we should not know that

that we did know that one, that is, that Conception would not properly be Cogitation, but would be, as toubhing without feeling. However, since there is so great a diversity of Objects in the World, all-around us, and consequently, so many various Impressions made upon the Mind, by those Objects, so that its Conceptive Power cannot but be diversly Affected, and moved, and the Mind also have a perceivance of that diversity; hence it comes to pass, that Conception is always Cogitation. In short, Conception is Modification of Mind, and Cogitation is Conception with Consciousness of it. Consciousness of Conception is a sense of the Alteration made in the Mind by that Conception (of which it is conscious;) *si nihil* (says *Cotta apud Cicer. l. 1. de Nat. Deor.*) *inter Deum & Deum* differt, *nulla est apud Deos* cognitio nulla *perceptio*,

I know very well that Monsieur *Des Cartes*, the ingenious *Honorato Fabri*, and many others do differ from me, for denying (as they do) that Sensation is Knowledge, and consequently, excluding both Conception and Consciousness from the Idea of it, they must also deny, that Sense is a Cogitative or Conceptive Power. But then, it is hard to say, what that Idea is, that they have of Sensation. Besides, 'tis

most

moſt certain that in Men, Senſation is Concious Perception, for whatever Impreſſion is made upon our Eye by any Object, we do not for all that, diſcern, or ſee the Object, if we do not atend unto, as well as receive, the Impreſſion; that is, we do not diſcern or ſee, but when we Know we do. Then only we have a Senſation of Objects, when we are Conſcious that they do Impreſs us; that is, when our Organs being Impreſſed, there ariſe and ſpring up in us, by means of thoſe Impreſſions, certain Images or Conceptions, that (many of them) by a Natural deluſion do ſeem as really to Exiſt without us, in the Objects themſelves, as if they were indeed ſo many real Affections of them, or Inherent Accidents in them. And thoſe Images being but Modifications of Mind, ariſe not in us upon any Impreſſions but when the Mind Attends to them, for elſe they cannot Affect it.

But happily it will be told me, that this Conſciouſneſs of Impreſſions, which is in men, when they do ſee, or hear, or otherwiſe perceive Objects, by the Affections of their External Organs, Ariſes in them only from the *Concomitance* of the Underſtanding; becauſe in men, whatevet Affects the Senſe, is alſo perceived by the Underſtanding; but that there neither is, nor can

can be, any such thing in other Animals, which are as void of Consciousness of any Impression made upon their Organs, as they are of that Reason and Understanding that makes it in Men. But as this may be said, so it may be as easily Replyed to; for 'tis as impossible, that Men should have any clear, or indeed any *Idea*, at all of Sensation, in other *Species* of Animals, but by that, which they have of their own; *as* it is certain, that Sensation in Men cannot be understood to be without Conception, nor Conception without Attention of Mind. *Attention of Mind*, is the Application of it unto Objects, and therefore in Men, is called *Minding*: Without Attention no Conception, and without Conception no Consciousness; Consciousness being (as I have said) nothing but a Sense of Alteration made in the Mind, by some new Affection of it, that is, by a new Thought or Conception. Besides, there are many other things that do make for this Opinion, that all Animal Sensation is Cogitation; particularly, that great *Sagacity* that is in some Animals, which cannot be accounted for with any clearness, but by allowing to them a great degree of Knowledge and Consciousness.

And hence it follows, that Sense and Imagination, as well as the Understanding

ing and Reason, are Mental and Spiritual, not meerly Mechanick and Material Powers By Mechanick and meerly Material Powers I understand such as do result from Matter only, and the Modes of Matter; from Local Motion and Rest, and from Size, Figure and Texture. By *Mental Spiritual* Powers, I understand such as cannot be conceived to arise from Matter only, and the Modes of Matter, without the Influence of Mind; and in the number of these I reckon Sense, and Imagination, as well as the Understanding or Reason. It is true, the term [*Mind*] is Appropriated, by way of excellency, to the Understanding or Reason, this being a faculty that hath the participation of Mind in a higher degree than the others have: But yet, there is Mind, and as much of Mind in all the Conceptive Cogitative Acts of Sense or Imagination, as there is of Conception and Cogitation in them. Thus I have shewed how Sense, Imagination, and Reason do *agree*, now I am to shew how they *differ*.

Sense, (by which I mean the power of Seeing, of Hearing, of Tasting, of Smelling, and of Feeling,) is that by which we make acquaintance with External Objects, and have Knowledge of them by means of Images and Apparitions, or
(which

(which is a better expression, as being more General and Comprehensive,) by *Sentiments* excited in the External Organs, through Impressions made upon them from Objects. *Imagination* is internal Sense, or an (After) Representation of the Images or Sentiments (that have been) excited before in the Sense: This is the Basis and Foundation of it; Composition, Division, and Enlargement of Images, is but Accessory, but Superstructure, and an Improvement of Sense. *Reason* or Understanding, is a faculty by which we know External Objects, as well as our own Acts, without framing Images of them; only by *Ideas* or Notions. In short, *Sensation*, properly, is Imagination, for every Sense Imagines; and that, which commonly is called *Imagination*, is but Remembrance, or Recollection of Sensation. Imagination, is *Repetition* of Sensation made from within, Sensation, is Imagination occasioned by immediate Impressions from without us. *Reason* or Understanding, is refined, Sublimated Sensation, that is, a conscious preception of things by *Notions* or Ideas, and not by Images, or sensible Representations. And thus, *all* the cogitative powers that are in Man, may be reduced to *Two*, to *Sense* and *Reason*; the former comprehending the Imagination, which is but the

the power of Remembring Senſations, and of Amplifying them; and the Letter comprehending Intellectual Remembrance, which is only a recollection of Ideas or Notions.

But to make a Reflection of more light, it may be minded, that when we look on a *Book*, (to Inſtance in a thing that is next to hand,) and read any *Sentence* in it, as this, *God is a Spirit*, we have at that time in our Eyes the *Figures* of the *Letters* that compoſe the Words, and ſo do know by *them*, what the words are; and this is *Senſe*. But if putting aſide the Book we will endeavour to *Recollect* thoſe words, we muſt do it one of *two* ways; *either* by Retrieving in our thoughts the very Figures and Imagies of the Letters and Words before preſented to our Eyes; or (which we oftneſt do) by recalling the Words and Sentence, and ſaying to our ſelves, or unto others, *God is a Spirit*, without thinking in the leaſt, of any Figures of the Letters that do make the Words, or of the Images of the Words that compoſe the Sentence. In the former we do *Imagine* the Sentence, as raiſing again the Images of the Words that make it, and this is *Senſible* Remembrance; but in the latter, though, when we Recollect the Sentence, we muſt withal (ſome way

or

or other) mind again the words that compose it, yet we do it *without* Imagining them, and this is *Intellectual* Remembrance, or the act of the Reason. Add, that at the same time that we do see the Schemes and Figures of the Letters, and have the portraictures and draughts of the words presented to our Eyes, which is *Sense*, we have, or may have, in our minds the sense and meaning of those words, of which sense or meaning however, we have neither Picture or Figure ; and this is *Understanding*: In the former we have *Images*, in the latter only *Ideas* ; we *See* the words, but understand the meaning This power of the Mind, (of perceiving without Imagining,) is called *Reason*, because in those Acts in which it does converse with things by means of words (and those are most of the Acts exerted by it) the sense and meaning of the words is (as it were) Inferred and Reasoned from them. What I have said, suffices to make the Notion or Idea of Reason or Understanding conceivable, by men who use Attention, and do *think*, but nothing will be enough to explicate and set it out to such as cannot endure that trouble, but will swallow all things without chewing-

SECT. II.

SECT. II.

Of Reason as taken for Contrivance, Contrivance, what, Sagacity what. Reason taken but for Contrivance, not Characteristical to Man. Of the Imaginative Contrivance in Irrational Animals. An Instance of it in a certain Hen. Apprehension, Composition, Illation, Acts of the Imagination, as well as of the Reason or Understanding. Composition of Phantasms, how Illustrated by Mr. Hobbs. That Reason taken for the Understanding (in the Notion of Understanding setled before) agrees to no other Animal but Man. Of Prince Maurices Parrot. The Acts of Reason as taken for the Understanding, reduced to two, to wit, Apprehension and Judgment.

I Know very well, that most Men, and even most Philosophers do take Reason but for *Contrivance,* or for *Discourse,* which is a sort of Contrivance; and that Contrivance (a dexterity in which they call *Sagacity,*) is a thinking upon means to compass and attain ends; as first upon the nearest means, then upon the means to that, and so on till all the necessary means are thought upon. But those who
think

think so, (to wit, that Reason is nothing but Contrivance,) can never evidence that Reason is the Character or sole Prerogative of Man, (which yet it is commonly belived, and said to be;) since there is Imaginative, as well as Intellectual Contrivance, and Imaginative Contrivance must be owned to belong to Inferior Animals, as well as to Men. My meaning is, that other Animals besides Men, and below them too, have a faculty or power by which, after a sort, they do conceive the next means (though not under the Notion of a Means) to what they would have, and then the means to that, and so by a train of Phantasms, go on till they have found enough for compassing the thing which they desire and prosecute. I have seen an *Hen* whose Chicken ran from her through a little hole that was in a Gate, through which she could not follow them, into a Court Inviorned with a very high Wall, that being in a passion to come to them, first she looks to see if she could fly to the top of the Wall, which was the nearest way and means, but upon Trial finding that unfeasible, and spying at some distance a Pent-House, from which she was able to gain it, away she flies to That; though it was to go farther than before from her Chickens, and consequently, no ways

ways for her purpofe, but as it was a means to reach the top of the Wall, which was the nearest means to get to them: Thus did this *Hen* contrive for her purpofes.

The Inftance I have given is a fmall one, and in a Creature not remarkable as many others are for Acts of *Sagacity*; it is not an Inftance in the Elephant, in the Caftor, the Fox, the Dog, or fuch other fubtle Animals; and yet an Inftance ferving well enough for my defign, which is to fhew, that Reafon which is proper and Characteriftical to Man, is not meer Contrivance or Difcoufe. For this it plainly fheweth, fince it manifefts, that Inferiour fenfitive Creatures are Contriving and Difcurfive, and capable of making network of their Sentiments and Fantoms; and withal (manifefts) that Apprehenfion, Compofition and Illation are in fome fort, as well the Acts of the Imagination, which is common to all fenfitives, as of the Underftanding and Reafon, which is peculiar to men. More, and Nobler Examples may be had in *Rorarius*, and in others of the Moderns; and in *Cicero l. 2. De Natura Deorum*, for the Ancients.

The way how Phantafms are compounded by the Imagination, is prettily, though perhaps not adequately, Illuftrated by by M. *Hobbs*, in a Similitude taken from Water; 'Water (says he) when moved 'at once by divers movements, receiveth 'one motion compounded of them all; so 'it is in the Brain or Spirits stirred by di- 'vers objects; there is composed an Ima- 'gination of divers conceptions; that ap- 'peared single to the Sense. As Sense at 'one time sheweth the Figure of a Moun- 'tain, at another of Gold, and the Ima- 'gination afterwards composes them in a 'Golden Mountain.

But without determining that Images are compounded in the Imagination, just the same way as Mr. *Hobbs* has represent- ed, this is certain, a composition of them there is, and contrivance too in that com- position; and this as well in Animals that are called Irrational, as in Men, who may, in some measure, guess at the latitude and extend thereof in other Animals, by what they find in themselves, in common *Dreams*.

But whatever Contrivence (that Re- sembles Reasoning) such Animals as are called Irrational may have, certain it is, that Reason taken for the Understanding, as the Understanding is a power of percei- ving without Imagining, cannot be evi- denced to be in them; they may Imagine, and by force of Imagination, after a sort Contrive,

Contrive, but it cannot be shewed that they Understand, or that they do Contrive the same way that men do, who do it by vertue of their Understanding. The Contrivance (and consequently the Discourse) of Irrational Animals, is a pure Effect of Sense and Imagination, and performed only by the *Sequel* of Images, which Sequels is not properly Illation made by way of Judgment, but as (in effects of the Plastick) the Images follow one another by means of their *Congruity*; or of some other Antecedent connexion; wherein the Memory, which is the Exchequer or common Treasury of all Sensations, and the disposition and order of Images in it, serves to good purpose. Such *Animals*, as they have not that use of *words* that Men have (of which hereafter,) so they have not that Power of Understanding which is termed *Judicative*; a power that so Estimates, and Weighs and Ballances Things, and their proportions one to another, by Comparing and Conferring them, that accordingly it pronounces upon them; *This* is *That*, or, *This* is not *That*, and *This* is *Such*, or, *This* is not *Such*; Which *Sentences* so pronounced, are called *Propositions*, or Enunciations, and are, really, *Judgments*. Whence it follows, that the so much talkt of *Syllogisme* of Hounds, (for so so *Reisch* in his *Margarita Philosophica* calls it, when he says, *In bivio, feram alterâ declinasse parte* Sillogizant *canes,*) is meer fallacy; the *Hare* is gone either this way or that way, he smells out the minor with his nose, he is not gone this way, and therefore concluding he is gone the other, doth with open mouth run that way, without his putting Nose to ground. All this is but Sensation, and following of the *Scent*, without any thing of Enunciation or Judgment; there is nothing of *Propositions, Major, Minor*, or *Conclusion*, in the case: The Hound perhaps does put his Nose at first where the Scent is not, and not finding it, turns another way, where it happens to be, so that upon turning being presently struck with the Scent, he follows it, with an out-cry; without putting of his Nose to the ground, to seek for what he has found already.

I confess, the story of Prince *Maurice* his Parrot is stupendious, and if no Illusion was in it, as none Appears; or that it was not an Effect of Witchcraft, which I most suspect, (the Country of *Brasill* in which it was Acted, (as all the *Indies*) having many Diabolical Agents, that work by Magick;) I should think it a very *Cross* Instance to my former Discourse. But considering it, as I do, only as an Effect

fect of Diabolical power, I put it in the number of the Extraordinary Events, with the Tricks of the *Divining Ape* which Mr. *Terry* writes of, in his Relation of a Voyage into the East Indies ; and then it may not be drawn into Argument. However, that thinking men may have an Occasion to employ their Thoughts, and to make an Impartial Judgment, I will tell the story as I find it in Sir *William Temples* Memoirs p. 57. Ed. 2. in his own Words, together with the Reflexion he makes.

" With the Prince of *Orange* (says he)
" returned most of the General Officers to
" the *Hague*, and among the rest Old
" Prince *Maurice* of *Nassaw*, who, as the
" Prince told me, had with the greatest in-
" dustry that could be, sought all occasions
" of dying fairly at the Battle of *Seneffe*
" without succeeding, which had given
" him great regrets ; and I did not won-
" der at it, considering his age of about
" Seventy Six, and his long habits both
" of Gout and Stone. When he came to
" visit me upon his return and before he
" went to his Government of *Cleve*, it came
" in my head to ask him an idle question,
" because I thought it not very likely for
" me to see him again, and I had a mind
" to Kown from his own Mouth the Ac-
" count of a common but much credited

' story,

"ſtory, that I had heard ſo often from
" many others of an old Parrot he had in
" *Braſill* during his Government there,
" that ſpoke, and asked, and anſwered,
" common queſtions like a Reaſonable
" Cteature ; ſo that thoſe of his train
" there, generally concluded it to be
" Witchery or Poſſeſſion ; and one of the
" Chaplains, who lived long after-
" wards in *Holland* would never from that
" time endure a Parrot, but ſaid they all
" had a Devil in them. I had heard many
" particulars of this Story, and aſſevered
" by People hard to be Diſcredited, which
" made me ask Prince *Maurice* what there
" was of it. He ſaid with his uſual plain-
" neſs and dryneſs in talk, there was ſome-
" thing true, but a great deal falſe, of
" what had been reported. I deſired to
" Know of him, what there was of the
" firſt, he told me ſhort and coldly, that
" he had heard of ſuch an old Parrot when
" he came to *Braſill* ; and though he be-
" lieved nothing of it, and it was a good
" way off, yet he had ſo much curioſity as
" as to ſend for it ; that it was a very great
" and a very old one ; and when it came
" firſt into the room where the Prince was
" with a great many Dutchmen about
" him, it ſaid preſently, *What a company*
" *of White men are here ?* They askt it what
" he

" he thought that Man was? pointing at
" at the Prince. It anſwered, *Some Gene-*
" *ral or other.* When they brought it cloſe
" to him, he askt it, *Dou venes, vous?*
" [Whence come you?] It anſwered, *De*
" Marinnan. [From *Marinnan.* The
" Prince, *A qui eſt es vous?* [To whom
" do you belong?] The Parrot, *A un Por-*
" *tugez.* [To a Portugez.] Prince *Que*
" *fais tu la?* [What do you there?] Par-
" rot, *Je garde les poulles.* [I look after
" the Chickens?] The Prince laughed
" and ſaid, *Vous gardes les poulles?* [You
" look after the Chickens?] The Parrot
" anſwered. *Ouy moy & je Scay bien faire,*
" [yes, I, and I know well enough how to
" do it.] And make the Chuck four or five
" times that people uſe to make to Chick-
" ens when they call them. I ſet down the
" words of this worthy Dialogue in
" French, juſt as Prince *Maurice* ſaid them
" to me. I asked him in what Language
" the Parrot ſpoke? And he ſaid in Bra-
" ſilian. I asked whether he underſtood
" Braſilian? He ſaid, no, but he had taken
" care to have two Interpreters by him,
" one a Dutch-man that ſpoke Briſilian,
" and the other a Briſilian that ſpoke
" Dutch; that he asked them ſeparately
" and privately, and both of them agreed
" in telling him juſt the ſame thing
" that

"that the Parrot said. I could not (says
"Sir *William*) but tell this odd Story, be-
"cause it is so much out of the way, and
"from the first hand, and what may pass
"for a good one; for I dare say this Prince
"at least believed himself in all he told
"me, having ever passed for a very honest
"and pious man. I leave it to Naturalists
"to reason, and to other men to believe as
"they please upon it.

Thus that excellent Person. But to return, (for indeed, what I have said in this Section is a Kind of Digression, as being more proper for another place.)

The Acts of Reason (taking Reason for the Understanding) may be aptly enough reduced to two, to wit, *Apprehension* and *Judgment* : to the latter of which that disposition of our Conceptions into order and method, which commonly is called *Ordinative Discourse*, as also Argumentation and Deduction, which is termed *Illative*, and hath the name of *Reasoning* appropriated to it, do (both) belong, as *Instruments* and *Means*.

CHAP.

CHAP. II. *Of Apprehension.*

SECT. I.

Apprehension, the first Act of Reason. Of Words, the ordinary Means of Apprehension. The Ends and Uses of Words, 1. To distinguish things as they are in the Mind, in which, words do stand for things. Why Mind is called Understanding. 2. To express our Thoughts and Conceptions one to another. The Importance of Words unto Knowledge, in this second Use of them. Of the Sense of Words. Of Canting. All Use of New Words, not Canting. The Sense of Words twofold; Verbal, and Reall. This distinction of the Senses of Words Illustrated, and the Usefulness thereof explained. Why the Meaning of Words is called Sense.

Apprehension, or that Act of the Reason or Understanding, in respect of which it is said to see or perceive things, is the same in reference to this faculty, that seeing is unto the Eye: for the mind to apprehend, perceive, or know any Object, is the same (to speak by way of allusion and similitude) as for the Eye to see, or discern one.

What I have said in the former *Chapter*, does cast some Light on this Subject; but yet to set it out more fully, I will consider, *First*, the Ordinary Means the Understanding uses in its Acts of Apprehension, and those are Words. *Secondly*, The immediate Object of Apprehension, and that is Notion, or Intellectual Sentiment; Sentiment of the Mind. *Thirdly*, The two chief Affections of Apprehension, and those are clearness and distinctness; of which three considerations; the Second properly is a Subject of Metaphysicks; the Third of Logick; and the First is common to both.

Apprehension properly and primarily is of things, as things are taken largely, for (external) Objects of the Mind. By an (external) Object of the Mind, I mean whatever any wise is without, and thought upon by, it. Now, the mind may think upon Objects, two ways. *First*, it may think upon them nakedly and abstractly, as they are in themselves, (without considering them as marked and distinguished by Words, or any other Characters and Notes, that should betoken or signifie them,) only by having the *Idea* or notion of them. And this is to apprehend an Object *immmediately*. For example, without considering of the *Word* [whiteness,] or having the least thought of it, one may

consider

consider the *Image* of Whiteness, as it doth appear in Snow, in Paper, or on a White wall. But *Secondly*, the mind may also think of things, and consider them by *means* of Words, that signifie them; as when having in our thoughts the word [whiteness], we do not think of the thing or Image, but under that word, which stands for it; or perhaps do think and speak of whiteness, without having the Image of whiteness at all; for both *ways* we may think of things by means of words, since words may be used to call the Images or Notions of things into our minds, for else themselves may stand in our minds for these Images or Notions, and so may be discoursed of, or used in the Discourse of other things. This Instance I acknowledge is an Imaginative Apprehension; and I use it rather than another that is Intellectual, because the Understanding in its Acts of Apprehension, if not always, doth very often, summon in the aid of the Imagination; as also, because it serves well enough to manifest my meaning; which, in short, is, that the mind may think on things either immediately, without the help of words; or *mediately* by means of them.

Words are the Names of things, and of the Notions, Thoughts and Conceptions that we have of things. *Names* are Articulate

culate Sounds, appointed to signifie things and Notions.

All Articulations of Sounds, all Voices (for Articulations of Sound are call'd *Voices*) tho they be, or may, by composition and conjugation, be multiplied, almost to infinity, yet they are reducible within the compass of the Alphabet, and can be expressed by the four and twenty Letters, in their Combination; which certainly was an excellent Invention, and full of Admiration. For Words, as properly they are but Sounds, so, as Sounds they could not be spoken, and consequently could not signifie, but unto persons that are present, and within hearing, and to them too but for the present. Whereas by means of *Letters*, becoming capable of being permanent and fix'd in *Writing*, they become communicable, both to those that are present, and to those that are absent; even to the most remote, in time, and place. *Again*, Since *Writing* is a representation of our Words, as, Words of our Conceptions and Thoughts; so that Writings do signifie, and stand for, our Words, as Words do signifie, and stand for, our Thoughts; therefore when I do discourse of Words, I would be understood to discourse of those that are written, as well as of those that are spoken. And *in fine*, since thoughts
may

may be signified by gestures and other Signs, as well as by Words; (for there are *three* ways of discoursing, or communicating of thoughts; to wit, by *Words*, by *Writing*, and by meer *Signs* and *Gestures*;) therefore what I say of *Words* must be taken as intended to be equally meant, *mutatis mutandis*, of Gestures and other Signs (so far as they are used to signify our thoughts) as well as of words themselves.

The *Uses* of words are divers. The *First*, to be as so many marks and tokens upon things, to signifie and show them; so that every man may be able to know them again in his own mind, and to distinguish and discern them in it.

For the clearing of this use, it must be considered, that the Understanding hath not of its own, (as the Imagination hath) any *proper Images*, any Figures of the things it converses with, whereby to know or distinguish them; the only Images it has of things (besides those of the Sense, or the Imagination) are the *Words* which signify them; which do stand therein for the very things themselves. For to give an Example; There is no such thing in the Understanding as an Image, or sensible Figure, of Substance, or of mind, or of matter, or of colour in general, as there is in the sense, or imagination of white, of black, of red,

of

of green, or of other particular Colours: The *only* Images it has of these, and of all things else that are purely intelligible and mental, are the *Words* that signify them: Ay, the very *Ideas* the Understanding hath of things, are nothing but its definitive conceptions of them, or *definitions*; and definitions as properly they are of *Words* (which *Words* since they stand in the mind for things, are commonly mistaken for, and consequently miscalled, *Simple Ideas* of these things;) so they are made by words. To such a degree, in this respect, are words of use to the understanding, which cannot work without them; a thing so certain, that even the *denomination* it self of [*understanding*] at least in part, arises from hence; for the *Mind* is called (the) Understanding, because it has a power of seeing things *under* Words that *stand* for them; as well as because it has one of perceiving Substances under Accidents; and had Beasts this power, they would come but little short of men, as to Acts of mind.

But besides this use, (which is more private and particular, an use that every man must have of Words for himself) there is a *Second*, an use that men have of them one for another? to wit, mutually to express their Sentiments and Thoughts; in respect of which, words are said to be as *Mony*:

the

the meaning is, That words ufed to convey our minds to others, muft be fuch as are current, and in ufe, or elfe they will not pafs.

Speech or Language (the cloathing of our Sentiments and Thoughts in Words) is, in refpect of *both* the mentioned ufes, efpecially the latter, of fo much moment to *Reafon* (taken for Difcourfe, or Contrivance at large; that fome have conceited, that men are little beholding to any thing elfe but the *former*, for that degree of the *Latter*, that doth divide and diftinguifh them from Beafts. Reafon in their Opinion, in the Seeds and principles of it, being but as a Spark, which in men, by the advantage of Speech, becomes improved and blown into fuch a flame as has engroffed the Title; fo that tho the fame Principles of Reafon are common to all Animals, yet this *Improvement* of them (that only carries the Name) is proper to man, becaufe Speech is. And in truth, by means of Speech, or communication of Sentiments and Thoughts, as one man becomes affifted and aided by another; fo if we do add *Writing* and *Printing*, which are but Fixations of Speech, it may be faid, that every man is affifted and aided with the Sentiments and thoughts of all; and how much help this may bring toward the improving

proving of Reason, is nothing hard to be conceived by one that shall consider the great advantage a Consult has, for the ripening of Business, or making a judgment upon things, above the reasoning of any one particular solitary person; or hath observed the difference that Cultivation and Savagenes, do make, in men. Should one permit himself to imagine that Elephants, Castors, Dogs, Foxes, and other sagacious Animals, which can contrive and do so much singly, (as we find by experience they can, and do) should have the united Ingeny of their several Kinds; it would be hard for him to say, to what they might not improve, or to distinguish the near approaches that they would make to what commonly is called Reason, from the real use and enjoyment of it. Especially if he also consider, that Savage wild men, who want the benefit of Education, and of large Converse; so that tho they have the use of *Speech*, yet they receive not this advantage by it, do very little excel such Animals, but come infinitely short of civilized and well bred men; who living in great Societies, have all the furtherance that aid and mutual assistance can give unto them.

Some in regard of the former use that *Words* have, do call them *Notes*, or Marks;

and

and in respect of the latter, term them *Signs*; but in truth, in referenc to both their Uses, Words are *Signs*, since, in both, they do signifie, either to ones self, as in the first use, or unto others, as in the second. Words are *Signs*, but *Signs* that signifie but by agreement, consent, and Institution: For should any do it by *Nature*, the Language that consisted of them would be universal, spoken and understood of all, which none is: so that the way of tryal in *Herodotus*, of the most Ancient Language, was as ill grounded, as the Discovery made by it ridiculous. 'Tis true, *Jacob Behman* talks of a *Language* of *Nature*, but I think he rather intended by it the *Language* of *Signatures*, than that of Words; since the *Language* of *Signatures*, if understood, may be interpreted (as he affirms his *Language of Nature* may) in *Hebrew, Greek, Latin, Dutch, English*, or any other vernacular Tongue: And in this sense too, That *Adam* understood the *Language* of *Nature* (as he says he did) was a truth, and perhaps implied in the History, which tells us, That *whatsoever* Adam *called every living Creature, that was the Name thereof*. But tho this may be, as he says, yet I cannot believe that That is so which he adds, That *Adam* had the Gift [of understanding the *Languages* of *Nature*] which was lost by
hi

his Fall, restor'd to him by his Regeneration: For that the New Birth, that consists in renovation of the Mind, after the Image of God in Christ, has any thing to do with *Philosophy*, or the Knowledge of Nature, is a conceit that cannot enter into my thoughts: I do not find in the Holy-Scriptures, which can give us any certainty herein, that our Saviour Christ himself did teach, or that his Apostles and first followers did profess, Philosophy and Science of Nature. But enough (if not too much) in this place, of the Language of *Nature*, since here we are to speak of the Language of men, and the Language of men is words, which are not natural but only instituted and imposed, signs.

The use of words of usual and current signification is called *speaking*; the use either of uncurrent *Fictitious* words, or of current words *abused* from their usual common signification, to a private particular meaning, is called *canting*. Of the former sort of canting *Basilides*, *Valentinus*, and all the *Gnosticks*, in Theology; *Paracelsus*, *Van-Helmont*, and all the *Chymists* generally, with many others, in *Philosophy* and *Medicine*, are not only common, but justly noted, Examples. Not that the use of every *new* Word is canting, or that we need be as nice as *C. Cæsar* in *Aulus Gellius*,

and

and avoid a new word, tho necessary to express our meaning, as we would *Charybdis*, or *Scylla*. Words are but the cloathing of Thoughts, and therefore must be made and fitted to them; and if we keep (as near as conveniently we can) to the ordinary Rules and Laws of Speaking, the making of new Words, when none, or none so apt, are stampt already, to signifie our Sentiments, is a practice that calls for imitation, since *Cicero* himself has set us a *Copy*; many of the Words that now enrich the *R man* Language, and do make it so expressive, were Innovations of his: And *Epicurus* did so before him: For, (as *Cicero* tells us, *l. 1. de Nat: Deorum*) he either invented, or first applied the Word πρόληψις; *Sunt*, says *Cicero*, *rebus novis, nova ponenda nomina, ut Epicurus, ipse πρόληψιν appellavit, quam antea nemo eo verbo nominarat.*

The *Essence* of Words, if words are taken, not materially, only for Articulate Sounds, but formally; for Articulate Sounds as they are Signs, do lie in their *signification*; and their *signification*, (or that which is signified by them) has the Name of *sense* or *meaning*.

The *sense* or *meaning* of words (the want whereof we call *Nonsense*) is two fold; the *sense* and *meaning* of words in reference to our common ordinary *Conceptions*; and the *sense* and *meaning* of words in reference to the *things* expressed and signified by them: The former may be term'd *Verbal*, the latter *real sense*; or (perhaps to speak more properly,) the former may be called the *sense* or *meaning* of the words, the latter the *conception*, the *notion*, or the *Idea* of the *Thing*. Should a *Roman Catholick* tell me he means by *Transubstantiation*, that a real and substantial mutation of the Elements of Bread and Wine is made in the Holy *Sacrament*, into the very Body and Blood of Christ, but yet so, that notwithstanding this mutation, the *Species* or Accidents of Bread and Wine do still remain to affect our senses: 'Tis possible I may conceive the sense and meaning of the several words he uses, and also apprehend what it is he would have me believe, when yet at the same time, I cannot apprehend that such a thing can really be, since I see a plain contradiction it should; it being equally impossible to make a *Conception*; (that is, to frame a coherent consistent Notion or Idea) of the thing he means, and make all the parts of it to hang together, as to make *one* of a circular *square*, or of a Triangular *Circle*. *Ecquem*, says *Cotta* in *Cicero*, *l. 3. de Nat. Deorum pag.* 129. *tam amentem esse putas, qui illud, quo vescatur, deum credat esse?*

A

A *Diſtinction* then there is (and that a remarkable one too) between the verbal, and real, meaning of words; which to set out more fully, I will ſhow, *Firſt*, The the Occaſion, and Riſe of it, and then *Secondly*, The Uſe and Benefit of it.

Firſt then, this diſtinction *Ariſes* from the Imperfection and Inadequacy of Human Knowledge; we Knowing little of things but under words, and words being (immediately) the ſigns but, of our Conceptions, which are always ſhort and narrow, and, too often, indiſtinct and confuſed. Now if the ſentiments we have according to the Vulgar and Ordinary way of conceiving, which is but general and confuſed, do cohere and hang together, when one of them is affirmed or ſpoken of another, ſo that the Notions are compoſſible in common acceptation, we *call* it ſenſe, though really the things themſelves (for which thoſe words are underſtood to ſtand) be Incompoſſible, and repugnant each to other, and therefore *indeed* it is Nonſenſe. This is to be better underſtood in Examples. Such *Propoſitions* as theſe, that *Colours* (even as to their Images) are in the Objects in which they do appear; that *Odours* are in the things ſmelled; that *Sapors* are in the things that are taſted; theſe and the like Aſſertions are not commonly underſtood, or ſaid, to be Nonſenſe, becauſe, Knowing in the general and confuſedly, what is meant by colour, what by Odor, and what by *Sapor*, as likewiſe what is meant by the thing ſeen, by the thing that is taſted, and by the thing which is ſmelled ; nothing appears in thoſe confuſed general Notions (which we have,) to hinder us from thinking that Colours, Sapors, and Odours do as really Inhere in thoſe external objects, as they ſeem to do. And yet to a Perſon that hath diſtinct, real, and juſt conceptions of the ſeveral ſubjects and predicates in thoſe propoſitions, it is evident, that 'tis as groſs and palpable *Nonſenſe* to affirm that Colours, Sapors, Odours, and other Accidents, (which are but *Phænomena* and Intentional beings) do really exiſt in the Subjects where they ſeem to be, as to ſay, that there are Notions and Cogitations in a Wall, in a Figg, or in a Roſe, than which there cannot be a greater Bull or abſurdity.

The *Uſefulneſs* of this diſtinction, is greater than moſt will think ; ſince from the want of making, or of obſerving it, it comes to paſs, that ſo many do run into great miſtakes and errours, in their diſcourſes ; *Do* skirmiſh one with another, to no purpoſe, and without end ; and often

ten *do* differ from themselves, as much as each from other. For few there are that do fix and settle even the verbal Sense of words, (which often have a doubleness of meaning, and then are called *Ambiguous*;) and fewer that do think of the real, without which yet, they can never come to any certainty ; so that, (as Mr. *Hobbs* has ingeniously said ; words that are Wise Mens *Counters*, become Fools *Mony*.

The meaning of words, as well the verbal, as the real, is called *Sense*, because the Perception of it ought to be as *Clear*, and distinct, and as steady and fixt, as that of Sense is : For words, to be understood as they ought, must have their meanings be as clearly and distinctly perceived, by the mind, as objects of Sense when they are Seen, or Heard, or Tasted, or Smelled, are by the Senses.

D 3   SECT. II.

SECT. II.

All Falsity is not Nonsense; but all impossible Falsity is. Repugnance in the mind to yield assent to propositions that are Nonsence. Whence it arises. Of Enthusiasm, as it is a Kind of Nonsence. What Enthusiasm is. The distributions of it. Examples of the several Kinds of Enthusiasm, out of Dr. Fludd, and in the Magick Aphorisms of the Rosy-crusians. That Enthusiasts when they seem to understand one another, do so by Sympathy only, and not by way of Apprehension and Judgment. How this may be, set out in a story very Remarkable.

I Have spoken of Sense and Nonsense in the general; but toward a further clearing of the Notions of them, and especially that of the latter, it must be observed, that falsity and Nonsence are not Synonimous terms; For all *Falsity* is not Nonsense, that is, every Proposition that is false, is not also Nonsensical; for many things are *possible*, that are not *Actual*; and therefore many propositions that are not actually true, might have been, or may hereafter be so; and as what is true, is

Sense

Sense, so Sense is *compossibility*, not actuality; not that only which at present is true, but whatever is any wise possible to be so. But though all Falsity is not Nonsense; all *impossible* Falsity is. I mean, every proposition is Nonsense, that is false to that degree, that it is impossible (absolutely impossible) it should be true; for no proposition is absolutely impossible to be true but that which implies contradiction, and that which implies a contradiction must needs be Nonsense; since the Understanding cannot frame any Notion or Idea of it, and so cannot make any real sense of the words, that compose it. Contradiction in *Terms* is plain or gross Nonsense, (called a *Bull* in English, or an Absurdity;) and where the terms in common acceptation are not Contradictory, yet if the thing they are designed to express do really imply a Contradiction, the propositions, though Verbal Sense, are really Nonsense; as in the Instances above.

Observe again, that there is in the mind a certain sensible *Reluctance* to give assent to Propositions that are Incongruous, and really Nonsensical; for whoever Attends to what does pass within himself, will be Conscious of a *Pain* (as it were of dislocation) upon a serious predication of Abstracts one of another; as when he says, good-ness

ness is Justice; or of Contraries, as when he affirms, love is hatred, and the like in other Instances. The *Reason* is plain. For as this is to say, that one thing is another, so he that says that one thing is another, says also, that neither is it self, that is, says a Contradiction, and a Contradiction (whither explicite or implicite,) being Affirmation and Negation of the same thing, and consequently an Assent and Dissent at the same time, and Assent and Dissent being contrary Motions, or Modifications, it follows, that to say, or go about to Assent unto, a Contradiction, is to *distract* and distort the mind, and put it to pain, because it is to draw it contrary ways at the same time.

Nonsense in persons who pretend to supernatural Assistances, may be called *Enthusiasm*, *Enthusiasm* properly, is a false conceit of being inspired; to be *inspired*, is to receive immediate motions and instincts from the Spirit of God; the person that has this false conceit of his being immediately Instincted, and moved by the Spirit of God, is called an *Enthusiast*. A person may be an *Enthusiast* as well in matters of *Philosophy*, as in those of *Divinity*, and many Examples there are of both sorts of Enthusiasts, some of which I have touched before; but I forbear to say any more

more of them now, in reference to their *Original*, or the *Quality* and *Causes* of their Distemper, *&c.* Since now, it is not my business to treat of *Enthusiasm*, and to set out the *Nature* of it, under the Notion of an *Imaginary Inspiration*, so much as to speak of the *Language* of *Enthusiasts*, which usually is Nonsense.

And of this I find a full Example in Dr. *Fludd*, in the third Book of his *Mosaick* Philosophy, the first Section and fourth Chapter, when having cited the Seventh Chapter of the the Book of *Wisdom*, the 25th, verse. He infers in these terms, ' So that we may discern by this
' Discription of the Wise Man, what is
' the Spiritual Christ, who is the Wisdom,
' Vertue, and word of God, and how by
' his Apparition out of Darkness, that is,
' by the mutation or change of the first
' principle, (which was in Darkness, *Qua-*
' *si verbum in Principio,*) from Dark Aleph
' to Light Aleph, the Waters which were
' contained in the profound Bowels of the
' Abyss were revealed, and were anima-
' ted, that is to say, by the emanation or
' emission of this self same Spirit of Eternal
' Fire or Light, and afterward by his ad-
' mirable activity, and restless motion and
' penetration (for by *Solomon* it is said to
' be *Omnibus mobilibus mobilior,* &c. Sap.
' 7. 24.

' 7. 24.) It first distinguisheth and sepa-
' rateth the Darkness from the Light, the
' obscure and gross Waters from the subtle
' and pure, and then it disposeth the
' Heavens into Spherees; lastly it di-
' videth the grosser Waters into Sublunary
' Elements, as by the words of the first
' Chapter of *Geuesis* each Man may plainly
' discern.

This is a full Example, and yet in further entertainment of the Curious, and for more variety, I will add another in the *Magick Aphorisms*, (for so I find them called) of the *Brethren of the Rosy-Cross*, which are as little capable of real Sense (at least in my Understanding,) as that I cited before from Dr. *Fludd*: And I will give them in the same Language in which I find them, without pretending to the skill of Translating them exactly.

1. *Ante Omnia punctum extitit, non τὸ α τόπον aut Mathematicum, sed diffusiovum, monas erat explicitè, implicitè myrias; lux erat & nox, Principium & finis Principii, omnia & nihil, est & non.*

2. *Commovet se monas in Diade, & per triadem egressa sunt facies luminis secundi.*

3. *Exivit ignis simplex, Increatus, est sub aquis, induit se tegumento ignis multiplicis.*

4. *Respexit*

4. *Respexit ad fontem superiorem & inferiorem, deducto typo, triplici vultu sigillavit.*

5. *Creavit unum unitas, & in tria distinxit, trinitas est & Quaternarius nexus & medium reductionis.*

6. *Ex visibilibus primum effulsit aqua, Fœmina incumbentis ignis, & figurabilium gravida mater.*

7. *Porosa erat interiùs & corticibus varia, cujus venter habuit cœlos convolutos & astra indiscreta.*

8. *Separatus artifex divisit hanc in amplas regiones, & apparente fatu disparuit mater.*

9. *Peperit tamen mater filios lucidos, Influentes, in terram Chai.*

10. *Hi generant matrem in novissimis, cujus fons cantat in luco miraculoso.*

11. *Sapientiæ condus est hic: esto qui potes promus.*

12. *Pater est totius creati, & ex filio creato per vivam filii Analysin pater generatur. Habes summum generantis circuli mysterium: filii filius est, qui filii pater fuit.*

This it seems is the *Rosycrucean* Creed, in which perhaps there may be much of deep mystery and sense; but for my part I can make none, that is real; and I believe that
most

most of my Readers will be able to make of it as little as I; and therefore I have set it down as an Instance and Example of Nonsense, that Nonsense which I called Enthusiasm.

And here (since it may be demanded if such *Enthusiasms* really are Nonsense, and consequently unintelligible, how it comes to pass that *Enthusiasts* do understand one another?) I conceive it fit to observe, that when *Enthusiasts* think, that they understand One Another (as in truth they profess to do, and this so seriously, that 'tis hard not to believe them to have some impressions common to them, which may support their Profession;) yet for as much as no sober man, tho never so sagacious or inquisitive, can understand them, it must be reckon'd an effect of Sympathy, and not of *Intellectual Apprehension*; I mean, they understand one another not *judiciously*, by conceiving; that is, by framing clear and consistent Notions of what is said, but only *sympathetically*, by having, upon such Expressions, some Notions, and consequent Thoughts, excited in them, that are conformable to theirs that use the Expressions: it being with *Enthusiasts*, who possess the same Frame and texture of mind, as with *unison Lutes*, or other *Instruments* fitly tuned; in which to touch one, is to affect and stir all within a convenient distance. To

To evidence how much conformity in Body and mind may signifie to that purpose I will make a relation of a very credible Story which I have read of *Twins*; who exactly resembling each the other in all the Features and Lineaments of Body, and consequently in Frame and Texture of mind, did also *sympathize* to a wonder; so that being at great distance one from another, they would notwithstanding be stirred with the same Affections and motions. The Story is to be found in a Book entituled, *Remarkable Antiquities of the City of* Exeter, *pag.* 42, 43.) and is this; *Henry*
' *Tracy*, an Inhabitant of the City aforesaid,
' had a numerous Issue, being the Father
' of eight Sons, and eight Daughters; the
' the Sixth and Seventh Sons were of one
' Birth *Twins*, and so well like in a all Li-
' naments, and so equal in Stature, so co-
' loured in Hair, and so like in Face and
' Gestures, that they could not be known
' one from the other, no not by their
' Friends, Parents, Brothers or Sisters, but
' privately by some secret marks, and open-
' ly by wearing some several coloured Rib-
' bands alike, which in sport they would
' sometimes exchange to make tryal of their
' Friends Judgment; yet somewhat more
' strange was, that their *Minds* and *Affecti-*
' *ons* were *as one*, for what the one loved,
' the

'the other defired; and fo on the contrary;
'the loathing of any thing by the *one*, was
'the diftafting of the fame thing by the o-
'ther; yea. fuch a confideration, or in-
'bred Power or Sympathy was in their na-
'tures, that if *Nicholas* were fick or grie-
'ved, *Andrew* felt the like pain, (tho' far *di-*
'*ftant* and remote in their perfons, and that
'too, without any intelligence given to ei-
'ther party;)and 'twas alfo obferved that if
'*Andrew* were merry, *Nicholas* was like-
'wife fo affected, altho' in different places
'which long they could not endure to be
'afunder; for they ever defired to eat,
'drink, fleep and walk together; yea, fo
'they lived and died, for they both ferved
'the King in Arms againft his *Barons*; and
'in a Battle, the one being flain, the other
'ftept prefently into his place; where in
'the height of danger (no perfwafions able
'to remove or hinder him) was there like-
'wife killed.

The like (if not the fame Story I find
reported by the *Author* of the Book, Entituled, *England's Worthies* in Church and
State, Printed London 1684.. (*pag.* 165.)
who tells it in thefe Words: '*Nicholas* and
'*Andrew Tremane* fays he) were Twins
'alike in all Lineaments, and felt like
'pain, tho at diftance, and without any
'Intelligence given; they equally defired

'to

' to walk, travel, sit, sleep, eat and drink to-
' gether. In this they differed, that at
' *New-Haven* in *France*, the one was Cap-
' tain of a Troop, the other but a Private
' Soldier; there they were both slain toge-
' ther *Ann.* 1564.

These (two, if two) Stories open a great light for the understanding the Sympathies and Consents that are in the World of Nature, as well as in the World of men; but I think it not so proper to insist any longer upon them at this time, since the very occasion that I have taken of mentioning them here, is but incident, and indirect.

SECT. III.

Of Questions, their Nature, and their distribution. That a Question is neither true, nor false; neither Affirmative, nor Negative. An Objection removed. That proceeding by way of Question, or as it were of Inquiry, in Common Discourse, is very useful, as well as Civil. Judgment required in putting Pertinent Questions.

AS Words when they are *joined* and put together; for Example, a Vertuous

tuous Woman, an Excellent man, are called *Oration* or Speech ; and if joined by way of Affirmation, or Negation, are called *Propositions*, and Propositions joined by a Conjunction, a *Compound* Proposition ; so a Proposition when there is added to it a Sign of Interrogation is called a *Question*. For Instance, Whether the *Baptism* of *John* is the same with *Christ*'s? Whether the Heavens are solid? or Fluid? Whether the Sun is a Flame? Whether the Earth move? And since a Sign of Interrogation may be added to any Proposition whatever, it follows, that Questions are of as many *kinds* as Propositions themselves, in respect of their *Substance* and *quantity*; so that they are either *Simple*, or *Compound* ; *Universal*, or *Particular* ; *Indefinite*, or *Singular*. Only as to the *quality* of Propositions, as well the *Verbal*, (which is the Affirmation, or the Negation is in them,) as the *real*, (their verity, or falsity,) it must be owned, that Questions are not capable of the same distribution in respect of this, as Propositions are. For tho' *Propositions* may be divided into *true* and *false*, and into *Affirmative* and *Negative*, *Questions* cannot ; since he who only asketh the Question, whether a thing is so? or not so? neither affirmeth, nor denieth it to be ; and he that neither affirmeth, nor denieth a thing to be, speaks

nor

nor true nor false of it. And yet it must be confessed, that as a Question may be *asked*, there may be implication of Affirmation, or Negation in it; so that in this regard a Question may have the Denomination of being affirmative, or negative, accordingly as it is made: But this is but accident, and arises not from the *nature* of a Question, nor belongs unto it as such, but rather is contrary, and only springs from the *manner* of putting the Question. I will give an Example in each: This *Question*, Is not Jesus Christ the Son of God? may be called *Affirmative*, because, being made in that manner, it seems to imply, that he who puts it, would have the Answer to be, he is; and this is Jesus Christ the Son of God? especially as it is *toned* in pronouncing, may be termed a *Negative* Question, because it seems to imply, he is not. But then either way of proposing the Question, is not barely the *putting* a *Question*, but also a directing the *Answer*: For to make a fair and naked Question, it should be worded thus; Whether Jesus Christ be the Son of God? else it may be only verbally a Question, but in effect an Assertion. *Quæstio* (says *Cicero, lib.* 4. *Academ Quæst.*) *est Appetitio Cognitionis, Quæstionisque finis Inventio.*

E   But

But to leave a Difcourfe that certainly will appear but dry and barren to fome, and to refer fuch others, who are better pleafed with it, and with the like, unto *common Logicians* and *Summulifts*; I will only obferve, that in common Difcourfe and Converfation, to make Objections by way of Queftion, as it is lefs offenfive than that of afferting and dogmatizing, fo, being well managed, it is no lefs convincing and perfwafive. For this Reafon the way was much in ufe with the Ancients, efpecially with *Socrates* and *Plato*, who preferr'd it before the Method of Syllogifm, and Oppofition; and in truth, to queftion, fince it is not to affirm, or to deny, does not contradict, or put a miftake upon Any, but feems only a further Inquiry, rather than Oppofition of what is Affirmed; and yet as it requires a great proportion of Judgment, and of ftrength and clearnefs of underftanding, to do it pertinently and well; fo being done in this manner, it gains more eafily, and as it were by furprize. Befides, the way of queftioning is *broader* and larger than that of Syllogizing, which is confined to one medium, and which too is often ufed to divert and carry one off from the bufinefs in hand, for which purpofe it ferves moft excellently well, if managed with dexterity.

CHAP.

CHAP. III.

Of Notion, *the immediate Object of* Apprehension.

SECT. I.

That Notion *may be considered two ways.* 1st. *In general; and* 2ly. *more specially. Of Notion in the general sense of the Word. No Original Native Notions. Why it seems as if there were. The Notion of Apprehension cleared. Of Notion in the special and limited Sense of the Word, what it is. That the understanding apprehends things but inadequately, and under Notions in the limited sense. This evidenced by several considerations. An Objection against it removed.*

I Have spoken of words the ordinary, but instituted, means of Apprehension; I am now to speak of *Notion*, the immediate Object (some would call it the natural means) of Apprehension.

The word *Notion*, may be considered two ways, either as it does signifie more generally and largely, or as it is taken in a more restrained, special and particular sense.

A Notion in the general and larger acceptation of the word, is *any* conception formed by the Mind in reference to Objects; and so taken, is the same with a *thought*, or that, in respect of the Mind, that a Sentiment largely taken, is, in respect of the sense. I say a Sentiment largely taken; for instance; when Sentiment is taken in spect of the Visive Power, not strictly and properly for light, or colour only; but largely, for any perception that the Eye has, by way of sight, of things, or of their relations and habitudes. And since there is so great an Analogy between the Eye and the Understanding, and between the Sentiments of the one, and of the other, it will be an easy inference, that no reason can be given why there should be Original *Innate Notions* in the Understanding (as some imagine there must) that it may be able to apprehend, which will not equally *argue*, that there should be the like *original Figures* and *Images* in the Eye, which should enable it to see; and yet none will Allow of *these.*

But to show how It comes to pass, that there are (as there are) appearances as if the mind had some original innate Notions, which for that reason are called *Prolepses* and Anticipations, and withal to bring some light to the business of Apprehension, which

which (as to the *way* of it) is obscure enough, and but seldom touched to any purpose: I will offer an Observation very common, but (as it may be applied) very luciferous in reference to this Subject.

Every body observes, that if a Blow is aimed at the Head of any person, he will hold up his Arm to receive it, and keep it from his head, without thinking either *that*, or *why*, he does so; and this is said to be done *Naturally*, and by instinct; because, in truth, it is done without premeditation, and so at that time, without any actual conceived design.

And yet again it is certain, that an Infant will not do so, or any Child before it has been taught and instructed to do it; which makes it plain, that the doing so in those who are come to reason, is no effect of natural instinct, but of use; only the Child was taught to do it so early, that by the time he comes to the Age of Discretion, having forgotten, or rather, having made no observation, when it was first taught, or first did it, and upon what Motives, and doing it now *without deliberation* it hath the aspect of a thing effected by *Nature*, and not of a *custom* or habit.

In the same manner in the business of *Reason*, we may, and often do proceed upon on Principles inſtilled into us very *early*, and are Acted by them, without Knowing *how*, or *why*, it being no Effect of preſent conſideration. *Experience* confirms this, ſince we may be certain, if we do but attend to our own Actions, that, many times, we are carried to the Affection, or Diſaffection of things, and the Approbation or Diſapprobation of them, we Know not *why*, and yet all the paſſions and Motions of our Mind, have *Reaſons* for them; for all Effects muſt have *Cauſes*; but *theſe*, ſometimes, are ſo *early* graffed in us, and, at other times, ſo *unawares*, that we remember not they were ſo; and then the *Effects*, only being obſerved, and the cauſes lying deep, hidden and ſecret, we do call it *Nature*, or Inſtinct, though in truth, it be *Reaſon*, and habit, as much as any thing elſe is.

Again, much the ſame way we do compute or *reckon*; for when we uſe any greater numbers, either in Addition, or in Subſtraction, or in any other Arithmetical operation, we do it without any actual conſideration of what the leſſer particular numbers are that make the greater, for that we have done before, (perhaps long,) and conſequently are poſſeſſed of the *Ideas* (may I ſo expreſs it) without the *Images* of them. But at firſt, we had a particular Knowledge. As, when we Multiply and say, Six and Six is Twelve, and Twelve and Twelve is Four and Twenty, we do it without considering actually at that time, that six is so many unites, though at first (but possibly so long ago that we do not remember it) we did so, and must (do so) to Know the particular value of that number; and the like is of others.

And thus also with an easie Application may it be conceived, *how words come to stand in the mind for things*, and that when we have the *word*, we think we have the simple *Idea* of the thing; it is just as the Figure [6] doth stand for the number [Six.] And that when once we have had a distinct Idea or Notion of the *Number*, afterward, (without actual thinking thereof,) we use the Figure instead of it, and that as well, or better than if we did distinctly consider the Number it self. Now, words do carry the same Relation unto things, that Figures do unto Numbers, and both Words and Figures seem to derive the power which they have of standing in the Mind as Representatives, from the connexion they have, Figures with Numbers, and Words with Things; after the same manner as we hold up our Arm, or a Stick, to save our Head, with-

out

out thinking of saving it. For though the Action prevents all actual thought of the End of it, yet 'tis done for an End, in vertue of it its first *Direction* and *Use*. This Discourse attended to, and well digested, will open a great light into the *way* in which the Understanding comes to have Apprehension of things by the means of Words; and to form its Ideas and Notions, taking Notions largely for *any* Thoughts or Conceptions.

But besides the former Sense of the Word [Notion,] there is *Another* which is more Restrained and Limited; in which a Notion is *Modus Concipiendi*, a certain particular *manner* of conceiving; a manner of conceiving things that corresponds not to them but only as they are *Objects*, not as they are *Things*; there being in every Conception some thing that is purely *Objective*, purely Notional; in so much that few, if any, of the Ideas which we have of things are properly *Pictures*; our Conceptions of things no more resembling them in strict Propriety, than our Words do our Conceptions, for which yet they do stand, and with which they have a Kind of Correspondence and Answering: just as Figures that do stand for Numbers; yet are no wise like them.

To

To make this clearer, it muſt be conſidered that the *Eye* has no perception of things but under the *Appearance* of Light, and Colours, and yet Light and Colours do not really exiſt in the things themſelves, that are perceived and ſeen by means or them, but are only in the Eye. Likewiſe the *Ear* has no perceivance of things, as of a Bell, of a Lute, or of a Viol, but under ſounds, and yet ſound is only a ſentiment in the Ear that hears, and is not, or any thing like it, in the Bell, or Viol, or Lute that is heard. For as the Eye has no Perceivance of things but under *Colours* that are not in them, (and the ſame time with due alteration, muſt be ſaid of the other Senſes.) So the *Underſtanding* Apprenot things, or any Habitudes or Aſpects of them, but under *Certain Notions* that neither have that being in Objects, or that being of Objects, that they ſeem to have ; but are, in all reſpects, the very ſame to the mind or Underſtanding, that Colours are to the Eye, and Sound to the Ear. To be more particular, the Uunderſtanding conceives not any thing but under the Notion of an *Enity*, and this either a *Subſtance* or an *Accident*; Under that of a *whole*, ore of a *part* ; or of a *Cauſe*, or of an *Effect*, or the like ; and yet all theſe and the like, are only *Entities of Reaſon* conceived

ceived within the mind, that have no more of any real true Existence without it, than Colours have without the Eye, or Sounds without the Ear. Every person that hath the least Understanding of the way in which we do apprehend things, will yield this to be true as to *Whole* and *Part*, to *Cause* and *Effect*, and to all the *Notions* which are commonly termed by Logicians the *Second*; and it is as certainly true in reference to *Substance* and *Accident*, to *Quantity*, *Quality*, and those other *General Notions* under which the Understanding apprehends its Objects, though commonly they are called *First* ones, and in comparison of the others are so.

I have laboured the more to make the Notion that I have in this business plain and easie, because much of what is to be said hereafter will depend upon it; and now taking it for granted that my meaning is *Intelligible*. what remains, is to evince *true*; and this I shall do, from the very Nature of Cogitation in general, (as it comprehends Sensation as well as Intellection,) since that the Understanding doth *Pinn* its Notions upon Objects, arises not from its being *Such* a particular Kind of Cogitative Faculty, but from its being Cogitative *at large*; let us then reflect

again

again on the Nature of Cogitation at large.

It is certain that things to us Men are nothing but as they do stand in our *Analogy* that is, in plain terms, they are nothing to us but as they are known by us; and as certain, that they stand not in our Analogy, nor are Known by us, but as they are in our Faculties, in our Senses, Imagination, or Mind; and they are not in our Faculties, either in their own *realities*, or by way of a true *Resemblance* and *Representation*, but only in respect of certain *Appearances* or Sentiments, which, by the various impressions that they make upon us, they do either Occasion only, or Cause, or (which is most probable) concur unto in Causing with our Faculties. Every Cogitative Faculty, though it is not the Sole Cause of its own immediate [apparant] Object, yet has a share in making it: Thus the Eye or Visive Faculty hath a share in making the Colours which it is said to see; the Ear or Auditive Power, a share in producing sounds, which yet it is said to hear; the Imagination has a part in making the Imagies stored in it; and there is the same Reason for the Understanding, that it should have a like share in framing the *Primitive Notions* under which it takes in and receives Objects: In sum, summ, the *immediate Objects* of cogitation, as it is exercised by men, are *entia cogitationis*, all Phænomena; Appearances that do no more exist without our faculties in the things themselves, than the Images that are seen in water, or behind a glass, do really exist in those places where they seem to be.

But as this is a truth that Many will admit with more facility in reference to the Objects of Sense, and Imagination, as Colours, Sapors, Sounds, &c. Than to those of the Mind or Understanding, such as Substance, Accident, Quality, Action, &c. So I find my self obliged to give a farther *demonstration* that it holds in these, as well as in those; which I hope to do by the following Considerations.

First, the understanding converses not with things ordinarily but by the Intervention of the sense, and since sentiments of sense are but Appearances, not Pictures, or proper Representations, it is hard to conceive how such conceptions are framed only by their occasion, and only wrought out of them, should be pourtraits of the things themselves, and made just and exact to them.

Secondly, The understanding is a power of

of that nature that many think it doth not immediately Attinge (as they call it) or reach particular singular beings, which yet are the only beings that compose the Universe; as members or parts of it; and really, it uses to proceed by way of *Abstraction*, and therefore doth more Connaturally converse with Universals, that are not of Mundane existence, than with singulars that are. Now, since things as they are in the mind, do undergo an *Abstraction* and sublimation, certain it is, they must put on another dress there, and so appear in quite another shape than that they have in the World. In short, All Agree that our conceptions of things are but *inadequate*, as indeed they must needs be, since things have much Refraction (may I so express it) both before they come, and after that they come, to the mind; and if they are inadequate, they cannot be commensurate, that is, they cannot bo so just and exact, to things, as to show them as they be, and in their own existences.

Thirdly, It may be Argued from the very nature of an *Idea* or notion; since this after a sort is a sentiment of the mind, as a sentiment (properly so called) is, after a sort, an *Idea* or Notion of the sense; the
imme-

immediate objects of the sense are *sensible* sentiments, and those of the understanding are *Intellectual* ones; which they must needs be, because the understanding it self is a kind of sense, only a more sublimed and raised. *Mens ipsa* (says *Cicero, l. 4. Academ. Quæst.*) *quæ sensuum fons est, etiam ipsa Sensus est,* &c.

In fine, this is so certain a truth, that whosoever reflects, tho' never so little, cannot chuse but observe, that as he takes in nothing by his sense but under *sentiments*, which are the *notions* of sense, so he receives in nothing in his understanding, but under *certain notions*, which are the *sentiments* of the mind; since he knows nothing Intellectually but either in general only, under the notion of a *thing*, or more specially under that of a *substance*, or else of an *Accident*; and what are all these but *Objective Notions*? as will appear in particular upon the examination and Tryal of them.

Let us then inquire *first* into the *thing*, (for we shall shew it of *Substance* and *Accident* hereafter) and what is thing but *modus concipiendi*? a notion or sentiment that the mind has, of whatsoever any wise is, because it is? Thing indeed is the most *general* notion, but then it is but a *notion*, because it is general; and has the most of

[63]

a notion, because it is the most general. To be more particular; If the Question be asked, *what thing* is? or what is meant by that word? *Some* have no other Answer but this, that a thing is *that which hath essence*. But then it may be farther demanded, what is meant by *essence*, which is said to be had? What it is to *have* essence? And what is meant by *that*, which hath it? Or if it be said, that a thing is *that, which is*, (as it is by others;) the same difficulties again occur: for it may be demanded, what *that* is, which is? And what is meant, when it is said to *be*? And whether Existence be Essence? especially since Existence seems not the first conception of a thing; but is a second, or after-conception; as not being that, which makes a thing to be what it is, [a thing;] but what only makes it a thing in being.

By this, it plainly appears, that the meaning of the word [*thing,*] is but an *inadequate* conception, arising in the mind upon its conversing with *Objects*, and so doth speak a certain particular sentiment, which the mind has of *them*; a sentiment better understood, than defined by words; but a sentiment too, that doth not enter us into the knowledge of the Reality it self (may I so express it,) of *that* which is; *which* we only apprehend *inadequately*,
under

under the Disguise and Masquerade of notions. As, that it is *that*, which is; or *that* which has essence; or the like; but not by any adequate exact conception. And as for *Substance* and *Accident*, which yet are the first steps we make toward a distinct Perceivance and knowledge of things; what are they, but likewise *Modi concipiendi*? Entities of Reason, or notions, that (it is true) are not without *grounds*, but yet that have, themselves, no Formal being but only in the *Mind*, that frames them; there being no such thing in the World as a *Substance*, or an *Accident*, any more than such a thing as a *Subject*, or an *Adjunct*; and yet we apprehend not any thing but as one of these, to wit, as a Substance, or as an Accident; so that we apprehend not any at all, just as they are, in their own realities, but only under the Top-knots and Dresses of Notions, which our minds do put on them.

But here it will be told me, that plain unlearned men, who yet do exercise the Acts of Reasoning well enough, and perhaps in the best manner, as doing it without *Art*, and in a way the most agreeable to *Nature*, do conceive and speak of things without conceiving or minding of Notions, such as I have mention'd; for they conceive and speak of *man*, of *good* and *evil*,

evil, of *vertue* and *vice,* and the like, without conceiving or minding of *Substances,* or *Accidents.* But this is eafily got over. For tho' unlearned plain men do not explicitely and in terms denominate *goodnefs, vertue, vice, &c.* Accidents, yet fince they do conceive them (as All do) all things that *are in* a man, or in fome other thing, tho' they do not call them Accidents, yet do they conceive them *as* Accidents: And when they do conceive, or fay of a *man,* for inftance, that he is *vertuous* or *vicious,* or the like, they do conceive him to have *vertue* or vice *in* him; that is, tho' they do not think of the *name substance,* yet they do really conceive that perfon to be *one*; fince a fubftance is nothing but a *subject,* or a thing that has other things in it as Accidents; whereas in truth, neither Accident, nor Subftance hath any being but only in the mind, and by the only, vertue of cogitation or thought.

F   SECT.

[66]

SECT. II.

Inferences from the former Discourse; first, that human knowledge for the most part is but intentional, not real. The usefulness of this Inference; an Objection against it removed. (And yet) Secondly, That the immediate Objects of the cogitative Powers are somewise external to those powers; and this, both as to appearances, (which is sensibly demonstrated) and as to their grounds. Two other Inferences added; the first in reference to the grounds of the Doctrine of the old Academy; the second concerning the obligation we are under ordinarily to conceive and speak of things as they are in our Analogy, and do appear to our faculties.

I Infer from the former Discourse; First, that human knowledge (at least for the most part) is but Intentional, not Real; and that we have no Perception of any thing, (In any degree to speak of,) *just as it is* in its own Reality and being. For all our notions and conceptions of things, are of them under *sentiments*; the understanding it self (as I argued before) being

being but a higher and more sublimated *sense*; and sentiments (as such) are in their own *formalities* but *apparently* only, not existently, without the faculties that do conceive them. To be be particular, we have no perception or knowledge of any thing but as it is a Substance, or an Accident, or a Quality, &c. And these are only notions: for example, as to *Water*; we have no knowledge of it by all, or any of our senses, what really it is in it self, just as it is, and absolutely speaking; for we are utterly ignorant (otherwise than by Conjecture) of the Magnitude and size of the little parts that compose it; Ignorant of their figure and shape; and Ignorant also of the kind, and degree of motion they have; all this we are Ignorant of, and yet this is all that is Real in Water But as Ignorant as we are of what it *really* is, in it self, and absolutely considered, we have much *Comparative* Relative Knowledge of it; for we know it by sense to be fluid; to have some degree of tenacity or viscosity; to be moist; in a word, to have so many Qualities (for so we conceive and speak that all put together, do give the mind a sufficient rise to distinguish it, as a different substance, from Earth, or Fire; So that a person that has at any time had

the

the perception of them all, will not miſtake them afterward, one for the other.

But here it muſt be remembred, that (as I have ſhewed before) tho' we do not ſee the *reality* of things immediately, and juſt as it is in the things themſelves, yet by means of ſentiments and notions, we do, ſomewiſe, perceive *it*: as the Eye that ſees not any thing immediately but Light or Colours, yet by means of Light and Colours, diſcerns Gold, Silver, Stones, Wood, as alſo the Magnitudes, the Figures, the motions, the diſtances of things; with a thouſand other Realities, ſo the underſtanding diſcerns infinite Realities, infinite habitudes of things; not indeed immediately, but either under the ſentiments of ſenſe, or by means of its own, which I call notions; as of Subſtance, Quality, Cauſe, Effect, Whole, Part, &c.

I have been ſomewhat longer in the Explication of this Inference, becauſe to know the *nature* of our Knowledge, muſt needs be of great advantage unto us; and much relieve us in our Inquiry after the nature of Things; ſince it frees us from the confuſion, that our mind muſt neceſſarily be in, ſhould it take the Apparitions of things (for ſuch ſentiments and notions are) to be external and real Exiſtences. Would not a thinking man be much perplexed,

plexed, to make a satisfying conception, what that Image is, that he sees in a glass, or in water, if he was perswaded of its being a Reality (of Existence,) and not a meer Apparition? The like must he be, who takes Objective Notions for *real* Existences, and who confounds *Attributes* that are only Objective, and that do belong to things but as they are Objects with those that do belong unto them as they are Things, and that are Real,

However, it will not follow, as some have weakly Objected, that then nothing is Real; for tho' the Images themselves of Whiteness, Blackness, Redness, Greenness, that do *seem inherent* in visible Objects, are not really so, yet really there are Dispositions and textures of particles in those Objects, that, by the various Modifications which they give the Light, do occasion in the Eye, to which the Light is reflected, all that diversity of sentiments (which we call colours) that does appear in those Objects. The same, *mutatis mutandis* must be said of sounds, sapors, odors, and of Tangible qualities, and in proportion will hold also in mental notions. For tho' the very Notions of Entity, Substance, Accident, Whole, Part, Cause, Effect, and the like, do not really exist without the mind; yet as they do *seem*, Real, and some more Real than others, so *really* they have in things without us certain *grounds* or Foundations, that, upon our converse with these things, do naturally Occasion, or Excite, such notions and sentiments in us. But I will speak to this matter more particularly, because it is of importance.

First then, the *immediate* Objects of Cogitation, both the Sensitive, and the Intellectual, are, in *appearance, external* to their several faculties; that is, such Objects do so *seem* to be without their several faculties, to which they correspond, *that*, in appearance, they are either the very *ultimate Objects* themselves of those faculties, or, at least, do *Exist* in them, and upon this account are called *Objects*; for Whiteness *seems* to the Eye to be *in* snow, or in a white wall; and sound to the Ear, to be in the Air; a Man doth seem to the understanding, to be really a Substance, or a thing that is invested with Accidents.

If it be *Inquired* how it comes to pass, that sentiments and notions, which really are not in the things that are without us, do yet appear as if they were, and consequently that they seem to be Objects? it must be *Answered*, that this arises from the very nature of cogitation it self, and of the

the cogitative faculties; and that both Reason and Experience do evidence, it must be so.

First, *Reason* sheweth that it must be so; for as we are conscious that we have a perceivance of Objects under certain Images, and Notions, so we are *not* conscious of any Action by which our faculties should make those Images or Notions; and therefore being sensible that we are Affected with such Images, and Notions, so long *as*, and no longer *than* we do Attend to things without us, (which things are therefore called *Objects*;) and not being sensible that we are so by any Action from within our selves, it cannot but appear unto us that we are Affected *only* from the things without us, and so, what really is only in our selves, must *seem* to come from those things, and consequently to be really in them.

Experience also shews; (to wit, that what is *really* but in the cogitative faculty, does yet *seem* without it;) for if the Eye by any accident becomes infected with *Colours*, as, (to instance in a more received, than often experienced, Matter,) with *yellow*, by the yellow Jaundice, or with *Green*, (as I have sometimes observed, before the coming of Convulsions;) that is,

(for

(for this is the Reality) if the Visive Spirits, or whatever other parts of the Eye, that are immediately concerned in the Act of Vision, be Preter-naturally put into the same motions with those, which by the Impressions of Yellow or Green Objects they are naturally put into, in either of these Cases, the *Object* beheld by *that* Eye, will appear as yellow, or green, tho' to every bodies else, it is but White, or Red, or of some other colour. And whence comes this, but hence? that the Images conceived in the Eye, (for in the Instances alledged, the Images of yellow and green are no where else,) are naturally *pinned* upon the Object. As is farther evident in *Dazling*; which is, when an Impression made upon the Eye by one Object, becomes translated to another; thus, coming out of a bright Sun-shine, on a Summers day, into a darkish room, one sees a *splendor* in every corner, and upon every Object. The like Appearance there is, upon the beholding of Objects thro' tinctur'd *Glasses*: So that it must be concluded, that the immediate Objects of cogitation, I mean the very Images and sentiments that are perceived, do, to all *appearance*, seem as external to the cogitative powers, as even the ultimate Objects themselves, that are perceived

perceived under them; which was the first thing to be shewed.

The second point to be shewed is, that the immediate Objects of cogitation are external in their *ground*, as well as in appearance, and in truth, are therefore external in appearance, because they are so *really* in their grounds. And this is as certain, as that every Effect must have a Cause. For *things without us*, are the Causes that do excite such Images and Notions *in* us: In the order of Nature, we do *see* a thing so long *as*, and no longer *than*, we keep our Eye upon it; and therefore that we do see it, must come from some *impression* from the Thing; and since to *see* a thing, is nothing but to have some Image *from* it, and so *of* it, in the Eye, and the Image is as the Impression, and the Impression as the Thing that makes it, it follows that the *grounds* of the Image is in the Thing without us. And since the Image (by which I mean Light or Colour) is the immediate object of *Vision*, and, that what is instanced in one Act of cogitation, will equally hold in all, it follows, that the immediate Objects of all other cogitations, as well as of vision, are ordinarily and naturally as external in their *grounds*, as in *appearance*; that is, are fundamentally external, as well as apparently.

I thought once to have ended this Chapter here, but now before I do so, I will add an Inference or two from the former Doctrine; the first is, that we learn from it the *Foundation* of that Opinion the *Academicks* of old were in, That *no judgment could be made of Truth*; that things do seem to us, but cannot be perceived by us; and that no *certainty*, but great *probability* only, is to be Attained unto by men. For as this Opinion had all the *Phænomena* of cogitation to give it countenance, so those *Philosophers* saw it; for they evidently perceived, that they saw not the Realities, but only the Appearances of things; *Plato* the chief of them, one of the most penetrating, as well as the most elegant, of all that ever were, affirmed that the present, was a word, of *Veri similitude only*, and not of Truth and Reality; That the beings in this World were only *Shadows*, but that the *Substances* themselves were in the *Ideal*. How far herein he went with the Truth, may easily be perceived by what I have discoursed before, concerning the Nature of Cogitation; as also, where he strikes out.

The *Second* Inference is; That since Sentiments, and Notions bottomed upon Realities, do seem; the former to the Sense, the latter to the Understanding, to be Realities; and since we are obliged to conceive,

ceive, and fpeak, of things, ordinarily and popularly (for all are not Philofophers) in that way and manner that they feem to be; it follows, that we are obliged to conceive, and fpeak of Sentiments and Notions in Common Converfation, and to the people, *as if* really they were the things themfelves that are perceived; or at leaft were in them: And fo may fay, the Snow is white, the Emerald is green, and the like.

CHAP.

CHAP. IV.

Of the distribution of Notions in the Restrained sense of the Word.

SECT. I.

Notions are either the Notions of things, or Notions about things Of the Notions of things And first of Entity or Thing. The Pinax Entium, or general Table of things. Things are either Real, or Cogitable. And these either meer Cogitables, or real Cogitables. A Reality what A Cogitable what. Of Real Cogitables. Real Cogitables, either Proper, or Reductive. Proper Real Cogitables of two sorts; of the Sense, or of the Mind. These of the Sense, of two kinds; Connatural, or Preternatural. Apparent colours, are real Connatural Cogitables. Real Cogitables of the Mind, like those of the Sense, of two Kinds; Connatural, or Preternatural. Real Cogitables Reductive, subdivided into those of sense (External, Internal) and those of the Understanding.

Notions taken in the limited Sense of the word, for *Objective Ideas*, by
and

and under which the Understanding apprehends, and conceives, of, things, and which, for this reason, may be called *Fundamental* (as being essential to the business of Knowledge,) are either Notions of things; such as Entity, Reality, *&c.* Or Notions about Things, such as whole, part, cause, effect, *&c.* of which the former are conceived as *absolute*, the latter more as *relative* Notions.

The Notions, (or *Modi concipiendi*, that I call the Notions) of things, may be reduced to four, to Entity or thing, Reality, Substance and Accident.

Entity or *thing* is taken in several senses; either first, in the largest, in which it is the same with *something*, or *Aliquid*. Or 2dly. more strictly, as it comprehends *but* substances, Accidents and Modes. Or 3dly. Most strictly, as it stands for *Substances* only. I take it not at this time in the *largest* Sense.

Thing in the largest Sense, is that which any wise *is*, or that is Knowable, directly: for Nothing, no wise is, nor is Knowable, but indirectly, and by means of thing, of which it is a Negation; Nothing is Not a thing.

And

And thing, or Entity, taken in the largest sense for

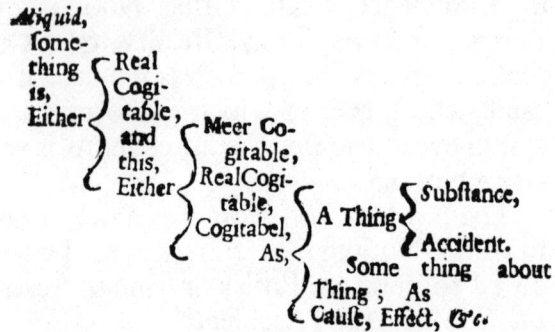

For that which any wise *is*, is either without the thinking of any one upon it; or it is no longer than while one is a thinking, and because he is a thinking, on it.

That which is without the thinking of any one upon it, and whether it be minded or no, is a *real* Thing, or a Reality; a thing that so is in the world, as that it is a part, or Appurtenance of it, and such a thing is *matter*, and every Affection, and every System of matter; and such a thing also is Mind.

That which no longer is than while one is a thinking, and because he is a thinking, on it; [so that tho it have that which is
called

called in the Schools an objective being, a being in the Cogitative Faculties, yet hath none without them in the World:] this I name a *Cogitable*; a Cogitable thing, or Entity. And thus, all the *Sentiments* of Sense, those of the Mind, and even meer Objective Notions, are Things, not things of Mundane and External Existence, but of Cogitation and Notion; Intentional, not Real things. For such are Colours, Sounds, Sapors, Time, Place, Substance, Accident, Cause, Effect; &c. they are *Intentional* things, things that, as such, have only an *esse Objectivum*, an *esse Cogitatum*, as the Schoolmen phrase it.

Cogitables, or Things that have being only in the Faculties that apprehend them, and by vertue of their being apprehended, are of *two* sorts; For either they have a being in *Faculties* by means of the Impressions made upon *them* from external Objects, and consequently have *Grounds* and Foundations in the things that are without us; or, they have a being in our Faculties, only by a working of the Faculties themselves, without any such Grounds.

Those Cogitables, that have being by means of Impressions made upon our Faculties, by External Objects, I call *Real Cogitables*; Cogitables, because the being which they have, is, *formally* a being in Cogita-

Cogitation only; Real Cogitables, because they have Grounds and Foundations, in things that are Real. Thus the *Sentiments* of Sense, such as Colours, Sounds, &c. the *Fundamental Notions* of Mind, those of things, and those *about* them, such as Substance, Accident, Cause, Effect, Whole, Part, &c. are Real Cogitables; Cogitables, for that the very Images themselves, the very *Ideas*, are Entities only of Cogitation, as having but an *esse cognitum*; and Real Cogitables, because they have *Grounds*, in things that are Real; for, antecedently to any Operation of the mind concerning these Cogitables, there do really exist, in the world, Things that in their own natures are fitted to produce, or to occasion them in our Faculties, in a certain correspondence to themselves.

Real Cogitables are either properly *so, or but* reductively.

Real Cogitables *proper*, are such things as have being in our Faculties, by the impressions of External Causes, that are *Objects*, as well as Causes, of the Acts that make those Cogitables. And these are of two sorts. For Example, (for things of this nature are best conceived in Examples) there is *Greenness* in Grass, as also in an Emerauld,

merauld, and there is *Bowedness* in an Oar, or a *Staff*, that is in the Water, so, as that part of it is in, part out: Now *both these* [the *Greens* and the *Bowedness*] are but Appearances, or *Pœnomena*; and having equally (one as much as another) their Grounds and Foundations in the things that are external to our Faculties, both are *equally* Real; and yet every one that considers must Acknowledge, that they are of very different natures, and that Bowedness is Not, in all respects, of the same sort of Appearance that Green is, as to its General Nature.

The differences that are in such Appearances, depend upon the differences that are in their *Grounds*, and therefore must be accounted for from these.

Some Appearances there are, that do *Arise* from sensation (for I will begin with *those of sense*) when it is made with all the Conditions and Circumstances that are Requisite, to make it *Right*; and these I call *Connatural* Appearances; such as the *Greens* in Grass, or in an Emerauld: But there are others that arise from sensation when it is not made with all the Conditions and Circumstances that are requisite to its being right and natural; as, when Vision is made thro' a double *Medium*, a thicker and a thinner; and these Appearances I call *Preternatural*,

ternatural, of which sort is that of *Bowedness* in the Oar, or Staff. These Appearances I call, the former Connatural, the latter Preternatural; not in reference to Nature as it is taken for the complex of all, or any, Causes; (for in relation to their proper Causes, all Effects are equally natural;) but as Nature is taken in a more restrained special sense (of which more hereafter) for a certain *particular* order of Causes and Effects.

As for the Colours in a *Rainbow*; those of a *Pigeons neck*, and others of like nature, *tho'* they are commonly call'd *Apparent* and Emphatical, and by that Denomination distinguished in *School Philosophy*, from those that are Real and Existent; yet I think not fit to make another *Classis* for them. For those fugitive *changeable* Colours, tho' they are not so fix'd and permanent as others are, yet they are as Real, and as Connatural as they; the fugitive waving Colours of *Changeable Taffata*, and those of standing Corn (while Green) Agitated and waved by the wind, are equally as real and Connatural, as the certain fixed Colour in Scarlet Cloth, or in Purple. Only, tho' all these Colours are equally Real, as having causes of their Appearance that are equally real, and all equally Connatural, because All (alike) are Results of sensations duly made, with all their requisite Circumstances; yet, since their

their Causes are not equally permanent and fixed, but some are more, some less; it follows, that some of these Colours are more abiding and permanent, and some but *Transient* and *Fugitive*; for all Effects must be, as their Causes Are. But to return.

What I have said concerning Real Cogitables of *Sense*, as to their Distribution, may likewise be said of those of the *Understanding*, that some are Connatural, some Preternatural: Those I call Connatural that result in the Understanding when it has all the requisite Conditions and Circumstances; and these *Preternatural*, that arise from the working of the Understanding when it wants at least some of the Requisite Conditions and Circumstances; particularly, when it is *Prejudiced*, or not well *Ballasted* with Observations, and Experiments, made by sense: In a word, there are *Visa animi*, as well as *Visa sensus*; and some of them Connatural, some Preternatural; of the former, every one that is well weighed, and well Grounded, is an Example, and for the latter, we have as many Examples, as there are ungrounded and senseless distinctions, and Notions; of which the Schoolmen afford us but too many, in their *Substantial Forms*, Inherent *Accidents*, &c.

Real Cogitables *Reductive*, are such as come from Causes that are Causes only, and not Objects as well as Causes, of the Act of Cogitation, which immediately produces them: And these as well as those that are proper, are either of the External *sense*, or of the *Imagination*, or of the *Reason* and *Understanding*: Since whatever is an Effect of Cogitation, and withal arises from an external Cause that is but a Cause, and not also an Object, of that Act, is a Real Cogitable Reductive, and not a *Fiction* only of the mind; and there may be such in the sense, and Imagination, as well as in the Understanding and Reason.

Before I give any Instances of Real **Cogitables** Reductive, it may be necessary that I shou'd explain the meaning of a Term that I have used to wit [*External Cause;*] by which I understand whatever is *without the Faculty*, and forreign to it; tho' in other respects it may be internal, as being within the Agent: To be plain, whatever the Understanding, the Imagination, or any of the external Senses conceive, by means of any Impressions, (even of Causes within the Agent, if they act without its *will*) is intended by me to come from an external Cause; and these Objective Conceptions, if they come from Causes, that are not also Objects, I call *Real Cogitables Reductive*.

In

In this *Classis* of Beings I do reckon *Dreams*, not only Divine (if any such there be) and Angelical Dreams, Dreams that are the effects of Divine, or of Angelical Impreffion, but alfo ordinary Dreams; as alfo the *Vifions* of the Feaverifh, the Melancholly, and the Hyfterical: And here likewife I reckon that Appearances in our ears, of the *Ringing* of Bells, which is only made by Agitation of the Internal Air, as alfo thofe *Sparkles* as of Fire, that do appear to the eye, upon a fmart percuffion or fhaking of the Fibres of the Optick Nerves, either by a vehement Agitation of the fpirits within, or a violent Stroke, or a ftrong Frication of the eye from without.

SECT. II.

Of meer Cogitables, or Fictions. What a Fiction is. That all Fictions are Creatures either of the Mind, or of the Internal Sense; None made by the External Senses. The Reason of it. Two Philosophical Doctrines observed, one concerning meer Cogitables, the other about Real Cogitables Reductive. Why the Representations of things in Prophetical Dreams, are always made as if they were present.

ALL that I have said already, relates to things that are in our Faculties, by virtue of impressions made upon them from External Causes, which Causes are either Causes and also Objects, or Causes only and not Objects; there are others that do arise in us from the working of our Faculties, (of themselves,) without any grounds for it, in any thing that is external, either as a Cause, or as an Object; and these I call *meer Cogitables*, or *Fictions*; such as an *Hirco-cervus*, or a *Chimæra*, a Golden Mountain, and the like.

Fictions are all forged, either by the *Mind* and Understanding, or by the *Imagination*

gination and internal Senſe; there are none in the external, the Eye, the Ear, or the like; and the *Reaſon* is evident, for Fictions are voluntary things, things that have always ſomething of the *Will* in them, and therefore cannot be created by any Faculty but That, which is under the Empire of the Will, which the External Senſes are not, but the other Powers are: For though we may think, and alſo imagine, what we will, we cannot See, or Hear, or Taſte, or Smell, or Feel, what we will. The Reaſon of which difference may be this, that if the Underſtanding, and Imagination, were not ſome wiſe under the power of the Will, there could be no *Diſcourſe*; and if the External Senſes were ſo ſo too, there could be no *certainty*; and therefore that there may be both Diſcourſe and certainty, our Faculties are ſo contrived, and ſo ordered, with excellent Wiſdom.

Here it muſt be obſerved,

(1) That there is *ſome* Reality even in *meer* Cogitables, (not indeed the ſame that is in thoſe that are *real*, which have a reality of Grounds and Foundations; but a reality) both in reſpect of the Cogitative *Act*, which doth produce them, and of that Cogitable and Objective *Exiſtence*, which they have in the Mind;

ſince

since it is as truly said, that one does think, or conceive such things, as it is of him that Dreams, or sees a Vision, that he does Dream, or see a Vision. Wherefore such Cogitables as these, in respect of their Objective Existence, may be referred to Realities of *Appearance*, as Dreams and Visions are; for as the Act of Dreaming Really *is*, and the thing Dreamt doth Really *seem*; so the Act that produces a Fiction Really is, and the Fiction also really seems. However, meer Cogitables, and Real Cogitables Reductive, or more plainly, meer Fictions, and Dreams, and Visions do not *agree* in all respects, even in point of Appearance; but as in some regards there is an Agreement, so in others, there is a difference, between them, in this point; for if any is to be made (as doubtless some is) between Real seeming, and a seeming to be Real; there is this between the foresaid Cogitables; that Dreams and Visions do not only Really seem, but seem to be Real; Whereas Fictions, do only really seem, but do not seem to be Real; at least not alway, and as Fictions.

2. It must be also noted, that in the Real Cogitables which I call *Reductive*, though their Causes are not Objects, yet they do impress our Faculties the same

way,

way, and with the same kind of *motions*, that Objects use to do, and that *such* Objects as do seem to Appear would really have done, had they been indeed the Causes of these Images and Forms, that do Represent them, in such Instances. Thus when we have the *sound* as of Bells in our Ears, and yet none are Ringing, the Internal *Air* in them, though Agitated only by a Vapor, Affects the Auditory Nerve the same way it would have done, had the External Air been really Agitated by the Ringing of Bells, and the Internal moved by the External. Thus also a smart Percussion of the *Eye*, Affects its *Nervous* parts the same way, and with the same kind of Motion, that a spark of Fire beheld by it would have done: And thus too in ordinary *Dreams*, the Spirits of that part of the Brain (if indeed it be the Brain) that is the Organ of Imagination, are moved by the internal causes of such Dreams, just in the same manner that they would have been, had they been impressed by Eternal Objects; which also must be said of Angelical Dreams, and of Visions.

And if our Faculties be moved by External causes that are not Objects, in the same manner as they be by external causes that are Objects, it can remain no longer a Wonder, that the Images and Forms excited in us by such Impressions, should seem as real, and as much external, as if they were excited by Objects, since our Faculties can make no difference. Hence it is, that in *Angelical Dreams*, as also in *Visions*, all the Representations which are made unto the Prophet, are as of things that *Are* in present, not of things that *Shall be*, in Future; *I saw a stone cut out of the Mountain without Hands*, says *Daniel*; or if a declaration must be made of somewhat which is to come, that declaration is made by way of Discourse, by a person present; so that still the Dream or Vision is *Narrative* and Historical; as in that of the Angel to *Joseph*, *Thou shalt call his Name Jesus*. Many Divines have taken notice of this Appearance, in the *Old Testament Prophesies*, having observed that these are always made in a *Narrative* Form, and as Representations of things present; but the Reason which they give for it, which is, that it is done to signifie, that the things Predicted shall as certainly come to pass, as if they were already, seems not so well grounded as the Observation it self; for I take it, the account that I have given is the more Genuine and Natural, which is, that External Causes that are not Objects do yet impress the Faculties which they

they Act upon, in the same manner that Objects do; and therefore all the Images that do Arise from such Impressions, must be of things as present, and in being; because they Represent them as if Really they were *Objects in Act*, that had excited and stirred the Faculties.

SECT. II.

Of Thing strictly taken, and of the Difference betwixt the Notions of things, and those that are only about things. Of the Idea of Substance, and that of Accident. Spinosas Notion of Substance, and that of an Accident considered. Maxims of Thing in general.

THing taken strictly, as it comprehends but Substances, Modes and Acccidents, is whatever seems *External* to any Faculty, and consequently, seems to have Being in the World, as a Part, or an Appurtenance, of it, whither it be really so or no. And in this sense of the Word, as *Real Things* themselves, (which are eminently called Things.) So likewise the *Sentiments* we have of these things, as Colours, Sounds Sapors, &c. are Things; and thus also, *Notions* are Things,

Things, both the more general and common Notions, those of Substance and Accident, and the more special, the Notions of the several *Species* of Quality, and *those* of Relations, &c-

But when I say, that not only things themselves, but the Sentiments and Notions we have of them, are Things, it must be understood with *distinction*; for the Things themselves, (so I call the *grounds* of Sentiments and Notions) are Realities of *True Existence*; but Sentiments and Notions being only Real Cogitables, are only *seeming* Realities; Realities of *Apparition* only, not of *Existence*: Thus, the *Notion* of *Substance* is a Reality of Appearance only, but the things that we apply it to, are Realities of Existence.

By the Notion of thing as taken strictly, we have a Rise afforded us to apprehend the difference between the Notions the Understanding hath *of* things, and those it hath only *about* things; for the Notions that I call the Notions of things, appear to the Understanding as *Things External* unto it; for (not to mention Substances) even some Relations, and Intelligible Qualities do seem to the Understanding, as really Inherent in the things they are Attributed to, as the sentiments of
Co-

Colours, Odors, and Sounds do unto the Senses. But for Notions that are only framed by the Mind about Things, such as Cause, Effect, Measure, Measured, &c. they seem not to it to have being in the things themselves, but to arise from its own Reflexions, upon comparing and considering of Things. Thus, at the same time that the mind conceives of Almighty God, that he is the Cause of all, as it does conceive, that the word [God] is the name of a Real Being, so it conceives also, than the term [Cause] is not, but that it only signifies a certain Kind of Relation between God and Things, as these do spring from him, and so is only the name of a certain Objective, and not of a Real, Being.

Of the things that do Appear unto our Faculties to have a Reality of being, *some* are perceived by them *immediately*, in their own proper Formal Natures, and those are either *Modes*, or *Compleat Accidents*; *Others* are not perceived by them immediately, in their own proper Formal Natures; but only by *means* of, and under, those that are perceived so; and *these* are called *Substances*: Compleat Accidents and Modes are Appurtenances, Substances are the things to which they do Appertain.

It

It is true, *Spionofa* is in another perſwaſion; who tells us, that he underſtands by *Subſtance*, that which is in it ſelf, and is conceived by it ſelf, that is, as he expreſſes it, a thing in whoſe conception that of another is not involved. Adding, that by *Attribute* he underſtands the ſame that he means by Subſtance, to wit, a thing conceived in and by it ſelf, in whoſe conception that of another is not involved. Thus ſays he, *Extenſion*, in as much as it is capable of being conceived in and by it ſelf, is an *Attribute*; but *Motion* that cannot be conceived but as ſomething in another thing, is None. Only he ſays too, to prevent Objections; that a Notional diſtinction may be made between a Subſtance and an Attribute, in this manner, that a thing may be called an Attribute in reſpect of the *Underſtanding*, which doth Attribute ſuch a certain Nature to a Subſtance; and then a Subſtance is the thing that the Underſtanding doth Attribute that Nature unto.

But as what this Philoſopher ſays on this occaſion is not very clear, ſo it is certain, that the Notion of Subſtance, as alſo that of an Attribute, is Relative; nor are the Inſtances he puts ſo well adjuſted, but that ſome exceptions may be brought againſt them. I can no more conceive
any

any *Real Extension*, than I can any *Motion*, but as a thing that belongs to another; Extension to the thing extended, as Motion to the thing moved. And tho' I do not believe my Understanding, the measure of other mens; yet I cannnot but think, it will be found on tryal, as hard a task for any other, as it is for me, to think otherwise; For what is meer Extension, but an Extension that belongs to nothing? And what is Extension that belongs to nothing, but an Extension of nothing? and certainly, an Extension of nothing, is nothing really, whatever it may be in Imagination; but more of this in another place.

Maxims concerning Thing in general.

1. Nothing can be, and not be at once.

2. Things that but Appear, do equally Affect the Mind as those that really are.

3. Things are not to be Multiplied Unnecessarily; as they are, when the Fictions of Men, are made to pass for the Creatures of God.

CHAP.

CHAP. V.

Of Substance.

SECT. I.

The Idea or Notion of Substance. Self Subsistence, how in the Idea of it. The Idea of Substance only Relative. Neither Extension nor Existence the Idea of it. Substances are either Principles, or Principiates. The Grounds of this Division. Substance that is a Principle, is either Mind, or Matter. Considerations premised for the better Understanding of this Discourse. The Ideas of Mind and Matter. The Grounds of the distribution of Substance into Mind and Matter. Abstracted Mind is as conceiveable as Matter, under the Notion of Substance. Spinosa's Notion of Mind rejected.

THE Primary Notion or Idea which we have of *Substance*, is (as I have hinted in the former Chapter) that of a thing which is a *Subject*, or an *Ultimate Object*; that is, we have not any Real immediate Conception of it, but only a Notional. Or (to speak more plainly, according

according to the Principles laid before) Subſtance as ſuch, is not a thing conceived juſt as it is in its own Reality, but a thing conceived under a certain notion; that is, a ſubſtance is a thing that is a Subject. For when the Underſtanding does think of the things we call Accidents (which are the only things that do immediately, and at firſt preſent themſelves unto us,) for example, when it thinks of Odours, Colours, ſapors, figures, &c. it doth at the ſame time conceive, that beſides *theſe* there muſt be other things that have them, in which thoſe odors, colours, ſapors, figures, &c. are. And thoſe things that are conceived to *have* thers, we call *ſubſtances*; as thoſe that are conceived to be *had* of others, or to be in them, we call *Accidents*: but what thoſe things, which we do Denominate Subſtances, Are, in themſelves, ſtript of all their Accidents, is no wiſe known; All we know of any ſubſtance is, that it is the ſubject of ſuch and ſuch Accidents; or that it is Qualified ſo or ſo; and hath theſe, and the other Qualities.

This Notion of a ſubſtance [that it is the ſame with a ſubject,] I call Primary, becauſe though that [of ſubſiſting by it ſelf,] is deemed ſo by others, yet, in our ordinary way of Reaſoning, and Inveſtigating of things, this [of ſelf ſubſiſting] is a conſequent one, to that of being a subject. For conversing with things; as the first that do present themselves to our consideration, are the Accidents of them; so the first Reflection the understanding makes, upon these Accidents, is, that other things are under them, which do uphold and support them, and consequently, that are *subjects*, or substances. But then indeed, when it comes again to consider, whether these subjects are also *in* subjects, finding in its self a certain Reluctance to conceive (that) they are, because, if they were, there would be no end, things would be in one another infinitely; therefore it concludes, that that, which is a subject of Accidents, is it self in no subject; that is, it is self-subsistent. Thus the notion of being self-subsistent, arises from that of being a subject: Nor is the notion of [being self-subsistent] a more Real one, than that of [being a subject.] For what is Self-subsistence but an *Attribute* that belongs to something else? but what that something else is, to which it belongs, I am willing to learn; and will ever honour as my great Master, that Person who will effectually teach me. We have no Ideas of any substances, but such as are Notional and Relative; that is, such as do arise from them as they stand in our Analogy, and are cloathed with Accidents.

A

A truth that might be made to appear by a full Induction of all the particulars; But will instance but in some; but those the most obvious, and most commonly discoursed of. For what Idea have we of *Earth*, but that it is something material, that it is fixt and tastless? What of *Salt*? but that of something sapid, and easily soluble in water? And what Idea have we of *water*? but that it is something material, moist, and fluid in such a degree, and the like? So that the Idea of a substance is that of a thing which is a subject; and this is a Relative Idea.

But many, who cannot satisfie themselves with the former, do conceit that they have found a Better, a Real, a Positive Idea of Substance. Of these, some do hold, *Extension* is that Idea, so that substance is Extension; and accordingly as Extension is either Penetrable, or Impenetrable, so they frame the Notions of *Spirit*, and *Body*; or the species of substance, as it is immaterial, or material. Others hold, that *Existence* or Being is the Idea of substance in general, and that substances of this or that particular species, are only determinate Talities of Being; for since in being is the Idea of an Accident, being (say they) must be that of a substance, and as to be is to exist, so *being* is nothing but *existence*.

I shall have another occasion hereafter to confider the firft of thofe Opinions when I come to Anfwer a certain Objection, touching the Idea of God; but will fay of it now, that thofe who profefs it, cannot make out (as they ought to do) a clear and fatisfactory Idea of *Extenfion in general*, that fhall agree in common, both to that which is Impenetrable, and to that which is Penetrable. *Befides*, it is not conceiveable, that a Spirit fhould be only a Penetrable Extenfion, fince (as will appear more fully hereafter) Extenfion has but little to do with mind or thought, which is Effential to a Spirit, and without which a Spirit cannot be a Spirit: and Penetrability, and Impenetrability has all as little.

Nor is the *fecond* Opinion more conceiveable. For not to Infift, that Exiftence properly taken is only of Caufates, (*exiftere* properly being [*effe extra caufas,*] and nothing properly is [*extra caufas*] that was not firft (*in caufis*;) I will take it at large, for *any* being in act; yet even fo, it is not of the Idea, or firft Conception, of fubftance: for [being] taken not as a *Noun*, but as a *Participle*, (as here it is taken,) is in the very fenfe of the term, a word of Relation; *being* is not a *thing*, but of a thing; not a thing, but a *mode* of it,
and

and confequently prefuppofing it; and that which prefuppofes thing or fubftance, cannot poffibly be in the Idea, or firft conception of it. In fhort, Accidents have being, tho' not the fame being as fubftances; but to proceed.

Now, if this is the proper notion of fubftance in general, that it is a thing that is a fubject of Accidents, it will follow, that we cannot frame any *Notions* of fubftances in particular, or make any agreeable *Diftributions* of them, but according to the feveral Accidents, of which they are fubjects. And this I defire may be noted, becaufe it will be of very great ufe in clearing what I fhall fay hereafter, in the profecution of this Difcourfe.

Of Subftances fome are *Principles*, fome *Principiates*. By *Principles*, I mean fubftances that are caufes of other things, but are themfelves uncaufed. By *Principiates*, (give me leave to make an Englifh word of one not very good Latin) I mean fubftances that are caufed, or compofed of Principles. Principles make, Principiates are made to be.

That there are fubftantial Caufes, and fubftantial Effects, in the World, is evident to fenfe; For even to fenfe, fome fubftances *begin* to be, and fome do *ceafe* being. Now that which begins to be, is made to be after having not been, must of necessity have Something, (and this something must of necessity be another thing,) that makes it to be; that is, it must have a *Cause*. So that Causes and Effects there are; else nothing could begin to be, or cease being. And if there are Causes, either those Causes, all of them have Causes also, and consequently, as they (as Causes) make other things to be; so, (as things that have Causes) themselves are made to be by others; or else, at least some of them have no causes, but are self-subsistent and uncaused. If all Causes have Causes, then an infinite Progression must be owned in the account of Causes, than which nothing can be more repugnant to the mind of Man; to Science; and to the Order and Unity of the Universe. And indeed then, there must be a number actually infinite, since all Causes are actual. But if any Causes are uncaused, (as certainly some must be, for the reasons Alledged) those uncaused Causes are *Principles*, or first Causes. More shortly, either something in the Universe of being is uncaused, and so is a Principle, for what is uncaused is a Principle; or else, every thing is Caused; but every thing cannot be Caused; for if every thing is Caused, Nothing must be the cause of Something. For if

every

every thing is caufed, every thing was once nothing, for what is Caufed was nothing before it was Caufed; and if every thing was once Nothing, either Nothing muſt be the Caufe of fome, or, (which in effect is the fame) nothing may become fomething without any caufe, than which No thought can be more unreafonable.

Again, as nothing is more certain than that there is fome Principle, fo the *Stoicks* (the Wifeft of all the Philofophers, as well as the moſt Devout) affirmed, that there are *two*, Mind, and Matter. Thus *Seneca* in his Epiftles (*Ep.* 65.) *Univerfa ex Materia & ex Deo conſtant.* All things (fays he) are compofed, or, do Confiſt of God and Matter. And indeed, we cannot be more affured by all our faculties, that there is *Action*, and *Paſſion* in the World, and that the World could neither be, or perfevere in being, without them, than we are to fpeak Philofophically, that there are *two* Principles, *one*, the Principle of all the Action; the *other*, the Principle of all the Paffion is in it; the former the *Active* Principle, or firſt fubject of Activity, the latter the *Paſſive* Principle, or firſt fubject of Paffivity; of which, I call the firſt, *Mind*, the fecond, *Matter*. This Affertion *Zeno* in *Laertius* fully agrees unto, when he tells us, that the Principles of

things

things are *two*, τὸ ποιοῦν ᾗ τὸ πάσχον, the Active, and the Passive; Nor doth the great Originist *Moses* say much less, when in his *Genesis*, he writeth of the *Spirit* of God that moved, and of the *Abyss* and Waters upon which he moved; and methinks, in all *Animal Generations*, in which there must be a *Male* and a *Female*, as who should say, an Active and a Passive Principle, there is some (and this no very Dark or Obscure) Adumbration of it.

Before I do proceed to a more particular Consideration of these Principles, I would have it be observed, that we ought to *Distinguish* what is manifest, certain, and of undoubted truth concerning them, from that which is but doubtful and uncertain. Now it is certain, *that* there is such a thing as we do call *Matter*; such a thing as *Mind*, such a thing as *Motion*; and *that* Matter is alter'd, figured, textur'd, and infinite ways wrought upon & moulded by means of motion. *Again*, it is certain *that* all things have not Mind in equal proportions, but that some exert the acts of it in a higher way and degree, and some in more ways for kind than others do; and also certain, *that* the exercises of Acts of Mind in all the ways and all the degrees of them in Corporeal Animals, (for we are not so well acquainted with others,) do much depend upon

upon the Nature and Qualifications of their Organs; that is, upon Texture and Disposition of matter. These things we are as certain of, as that our selves be, and have a true use of our faculties. But if we advance farther, and to endeavour to Enter and Penetrate into the very *nature* of Matter, into *that* of Mind, and into the *Nature* of Motion; here being forsaken and destitute of sense to hunt for us, we are much at a loss, and as unable to proceed in our search an inquiry after them, as to their just Realities, as we are in that of things, which are wholly out of our view. It is hard to conceive just what *matter* is in its own Positive Reality; also what *Mind* is, and even what *Motion* is, (as taken for a subordinate Principle.) Nor can it be Demonstrated, that (as some will have it) there is only *one* substance in the Universe, and that Matter and Mind are only several *Modifications* of that one substance; nor be Demonstrated, that *Matter* (for this I think they mean by substance,) is in its own Nature, a *vital* Energetical thing; and that the diverse *Gradations of Life*, that are observed in the several species of Animals, arise only from the several Modifications of Matter, and of that *life of nature* (as those Philosophers call it) which is Essential thereto, and is

the

the *root* of those Perceptive, Appetitive, and Motive Powers that do dress up being in all the Shapes and Forms in which it appears upon the Stage of the World. I will not build upon such *Hypothesis*; which being unevident, must needs be doubtful and uncertain, if not false. A Philosophy that shall be *solid*, and sound, must have its Ground-work and Foundations firmly laid; which none can have, but that which is bottomed, rais'd and built upon *evidence*; I mean, upon the certain *Testimony* of our faculties. And therefore since our *faculties* do rather go upon *Notions*, than on Realities, and do plainly *Distinguish* between Mind and Matter, and (as I will show in the Progress of this Discourse) do Contradistinguish them, I hold my self obliged to treat of these distinctly, but still in the *Real Notional* way

Mind then is Cogitative, thinking, or perceiving substance; or, Mind is the first subject of Cogitation. *Matter* is Extensive, spacious, substance; or, the first subject of dimensive spacious Quantity. In other, but Equivalent terms; *Mind* is Active substance, *Matter* Passive substance. I affirm, that these latter Definitions are equivalent to the former, because, in effect, it is the same to say, that Mind is *Active*, as to say, it is *Cogitative*; and the same to say,

say, that Matter is *Passive*, as to say, it is *Spatious* Extensive substance. Nor is Mind Cogitation, or matter extension, as *Des Cartes* makes them; but the former is Cogitative, the latter Extensive substance. We find a Reluctance in our minds to conceive that Cogitation is a substance, as also to conceive Extension as one; and yet we cannot conceive Mind and Matter but as substances.

The main Reason why I do *distinguish* Substance into Mind and Matter, as into *first* Original kinds, is, because (as I hinted before) Cogitation and Extension, that do Constitute their several Ideas, are of no Relation one to another, for what hath a Thought to do with a Cube, or a Triangle? or with Length, or Breadth, or Depth? Certainly Cogitation and Extension are quite different Accidents, without any thing in their Ideas, that is *Common* to both; and therefore the first subject of the one, cannot be conceived the first subject of the other; their subjects must be substances of quite as different kinds as themselves are, at least to us; since all the diversity we can conceive in substances, is and must be, taken from the accidents they have, these being the Characters by, and under which alone, we do perceive and know, and by consequence, can only distinguish them.

I

I infist herein the more, for that many think that *Mind* is only an Accident, and that taken for a fubftance, it is unintelligible, and a meer *Chimera*: fo that, tho' Matter is acknowledged (by them) to be a fubftance, it will not be yielded, that Abftract, feparate mind can be one. But thofe that think it fo, if they confider'd, that men have no conception of fubftance, nor can have any of it, but as it is a fubject of Accidents, they would foon change their Opinion. For the Accident of *Cogitation*, or of Activity, that Mind is the fubject of, is as diftinctly and clearly conceiveable, as that of Extenfion, or of Paffivity, which matter is the fubject of. Nor is the *thing* it felf that is the fubject of Extenfion, or of Paffivity; any more Conceiveable but by, and under *this*; that is, the fubftance of mind and matter are equally conceiveable, and equally unconceiveable. They know no more what *that* is in it felf, that is extended, than what *that* is, that is Cogitative; and may be as fure, that they do think, as they are, that they are fpacious, ay, they cannot know that they are fpacious, but by thinking. But of fpatiofity or extenfion, (the Accident that conftitutes matter,) I fhall have occafion to difcourfe hereafter, when I come to fpeak of quantity, I proceed now to difcourfe of Mind.

The

The Idea I have given of Mind, that it is the Immediate subject, or (as others perhaps would chuse to say) the Immediate Principle, of Cogitation, Energy, or Activity, is much more easie to be conceived than that of *Spinosa*, when he defines the human mind to be the Idea of a body, or thing, actually existing: for Mind, even the human, is not so properly said to be an Idea, as to be the Principle, our Cause efficient, of Ideas; since all Ideas (even in common sense) are conceived; and Mind is that, which conceives them. Thus it is in our Refracted, Inadequate, *Real-Notional* way of conceiving; and for an Adequate and just one, as it is above our faculties, so I do not find that *Spinosa*, or *Mal. Branche* after all their Ambitious Researches in that higher way, have edified the World thereby to any great Degree. This way of *seeing* all things *in God*, and in their own proper *Realities*, is a way much out of the way. Otherwise, when *they* keep the lower way of sense, many of their thoughts are surprizing, and excellent.

SECT.

SECT. II.

A two fold Consideration of Mind; one, as it is Abstracted from Matter; the other as it is Concerned with Matter. What is meant by Concernment of Mind with Matter- Of Mind. That is the Idea of God. God as pure Mind, is in himself, and directly incomprehensible. However, he is knowable as it were by Refraction, and Reflection; in an Hypothesis, and by way of similitude That a Parabolical, Comparative way of knowing God, ought to content us. Of the Divine Attributes; the true conception of them. The vanity of those who talk of seeing all things in God. Spinosa's Opinion that God is all substance Rejected, for several Reasons. That this Opinion seems to imply, that God is no singular self-existent, self-subsistent Being. The Ground of this Opinion touched. Another sentiment concerning God, that he is infinite Extension indued with Goodness, Wisdom, and Power, considered. The Ground of this underminded, and the nature of the Divine Omnipresence represented.

Mind

MIND may be considered, either in it self, as it is *Abstract* and simple, free from all Concretion and Composition with matter; or else as it is *concreted* or concerned therewith.

By the *Concretion* of mind with matter, I mean nothing but the acting of Mind in this or that particular manner, by means of matter. As it is in our selves, who do not see, or hear, or feel, but by means of Organs, that is, of matter.

Mind as it is in it self, Abstract and Simple, free from all concretion or concernment with Matter, I call *Pure Mind*; Mind Concreted with Matter, I term, *Mind in Matter*.

Pure Mind, is the Notion or Idea of *God*; as is implied by our Saviour, when he says, *John* 4. 24. God is *Spirit*; he does not say, God is a Spirit, but God is Spirit; πνεῦμα ὁ θεός, All Spirit, nothing but Spirit. In like manner *Seneca*, in the Preface to his natural Questions, first demanding what God is? Answers, he is *Mens universi*, the mind of the Universe; and being obliged, for the cleering of his notion, to show the difference between the nature of God, and that of Man, adds, Mind is only the Principal *part* of *our* nature, but the *whole* of Gods, which is nothing

thing but Mind God is pure Mind, all Reason. In his own terms thus, *Quid ergo interest inter naturam Dei & nostram? Nostri melior pars Animus est, in illo nulla pars extra animum.* Again, in his Epistles (*Ep.* 65.) He has this expression, *Nos nunc primam & Generalem causam quærimus, hæc simplex esse debet; nam & materia simplex est*; now, says he, we seek the first Universal cause, which ought to be simple (or uncompounded) for even matter it it self is simple. Only, I doubt, he (as many other Philosophers did) took God but for an immanent an ingredient Cause of all; which perhaps is only true of the Mosaical Spirit of God.

But *God* as he is *Pure* mind, is an *Inaccessible Light*, that dazzels all the eyes that behold it; and therefore, we can hope to acquire but very little particular knowledge of *him* or acquaintance with him, under this notion. But then again, as the *Sun* that cannot be beheld directly, in its own proper light, may yet be seen by Reflection; so may the Deity, in an *Hypothesis*, and by way of Parable; by speaking of him after the manner of men. The holy *Scriptures* themselves go this way. They Represent God as an Infinite Almighty Person, (suppose a man,) that hath Understanding, Will, and Affections; that
consults

consults and decrees; and that is touched (as men are) with the motions of Love, Hatred, Desire, Aversion; and in consequence of this Notion, do further Represent him, sometimes as a Father, sometimes as a Lord, or as a great King, that Governs the Universe, according to the Rules and Laws that he himself hath set, and by rewards and punishments. Now, all this is *Parabolical*, and but Comparative Knowledge: However, we ought to satisfie and *Content* our selves therewith; for though it is not to know the Deity in in the Reality, as he is in himself, yet it suffices for the Principal *End* for which we should endeavour to know him; which is to Adore and Obey him. *Besides*, it is well nigh the only particular Knowledge of him that we Mortals are capable of, in this Terrestial State; and, *in fine*, is almost as much, in effect, as that which we have of any thing else, even in the Corporeal World.

It is true we nnderstand that *Matter* and *Motion* are Real things, and that all others that are Corporeal, do result from these; but this (at least) is only a *General Confused Knowledge*, and *no more* than *that* we have of the Abstracted Pure Mind. For, as to the *particular* Natures of things, their Internal Fabrick and Texture,

I and

and that degree of Motion, that is in the particles which compofe them, of this) we have only a weak imperfect Conjecture, without certainty. All the particular Knowledge that we have of things by which we diftinguifh them one from another, both in reference to their Kinds, and to the Individuals of thofe Kinds, and by which we refolve their Operations, is of nothing (to fpeak of) but of *Accidents*; and Accidents are nothing but (as I have touched before, and fhall fhew again more fully hereafter) the *Sentiments* we have of things; *they* being not fo much as Grounds or proper Reprefentations of Grounds, but only certain *Appearances*, under which our feveral Senfes do drefs up things, and fo fhow them unto us: and this is enough for *Ufe*.

As therefore any perfon would know but little of this *Corporeal World*, and nothing ufefully, that would not take it in by his Senfes, and know it (as he only can) under the Mafcarade of *Sentiments*, that are not without him, but only in Appearances, and in their Grounds; fo, he fhall know but little of *God*, that will not condefcend to fee him in an *Hypothefis*, by way of Analogy and Similitude. What was faid by God himfelf unto *Mofes*, will hold

hold true in every Mortal; *Thou shalt* see *my* Backparts, *but my* Face *shall not be seen:* All our Knowledge of him at present, is but ἐν αἰνίγματι, we can but *Riddle* at him; the *Ideas* we have of him, are only *Attributes*; and Attributes are not Qualities really Inherent in him, but only *Notions* of his Operations, and of the various Relations and Aspects which they bear, to one Another, and to Us,) that are excited into us, upon the view and considerations which we take of his works. Thus the several Attributes of God, that we conceive and know him under, are, in reference to him, just as the *Accidents* of things Corporeal, their Colours, their Odors, their Sounds, their Tangible Qualities are unto them; we see him but ὡς ἐν ἐσόπτρω, as in a Glass; and to see a thing as in a Glass, is not to see the thing it self, but only by Appearances; and yet, he that will look behind the Glass, to see more, shall see nothing at all.

What, then, must be said of those, who think, they *See all things in God?* When God, though in himself he is Pure Light, without any Mixtnre of Darkness, yet, as to us, in respect of any clear, just, distinct Knowledge of him, He dwells in the thickest Darkness: No Windows

Windows in the *Sanctum Sanctorum*, where the Seat of God was; and the very *Heathen*, many of them, Adored him with *Silence*, as one that was Ineffable and Unconceiveable: Methinks, it is meer Enthusiasm, to talk of Seeing All Things in the *Original*, when we cannot so much as look upon *it*; God is Pure Mind, and Pure Mind is Pure Light, of too Transcendent Glory to be immediately beheld by us, but Blear-eyed, Weak-sighted Mortals.

There are *two* Opinions in reference to the Nature of God, that *Differ* from mine; both of which I will consider.

The *First* is, that of *Spinosa*, That he is *all* Substance, and that Particular Beings (even formally taken) are but Participations of his; as being only so many several Modifications of the Divine Attributes. But this is a Notion (of the Deity) that I cannot receive, as for other Reasons, so for this particularly, that it makes him to be the *Universe*, and to be Matter, as well as Mind; whereas, God is neither Matter, nor the World or Universe, but only Pure Mind; for
the

the Great World has a Mind, that made, and Governs it, as well as the Little. Even Mr. *Hobbs*, has said, *He that thinks this World without a Mind, I shall think him without a Mind*: And says *Seneca, Nat. Quaſt. Lib.* 1. C. 45. *Eundem quem nos* Jovem *intelligunt, Cuſtodem, Rectoremq; Univerſi ; Animum ac Spiritum, Mundani hujus operis Dominum & Artificem, cui nomen omne convenit,* &c. Which I would Render thus; God is the Father All-mighty, All-wise, All good, the Maker of Heaven and Earth, Soveraign Preſerver and Governor of All.

For my own part, I much doubt that thoſe Philoſophers, who profeſs themſelves in this Opinion, [that God is *all* Subſtance, or that he is the World,] do really believe he has no Being at all, but, only in Fiction of Mind, and by way of *Proſopopæia* ; and that as *Nature, Fortune, Chance*, which yet are ſaid to do This, and to do That, do, really, only ſignifie *Cauſes* ſo or ſo conſidered ; ſo, *God*, with them, is only a *Notion*, a Name, a Mode of Expreſſion, by which they mean *all* Cauſes taken together ; and ſo no more the Name of a Real Individual ſingular Being, than that of Nature, or Fortune. *Sunt* (ſays *Lucilius*

Lucilius in *Cicero l.* 2. *de Nat. Deor.*) *Qui omnia Naturæ nomine appellent, ut* Epicurus, *&c.*

The unwary Expression of some Theologues, and Theologizing Philosophers, who Denominated God *Nature Naturing*, might give occasion to this improper conceit of him, among the moderns; as might also that mistaken *Idea* of *Infinity* (as an Attribute of God) that some have given, which seems to shock his *distinction* and singularity of Being. For *thence* it is Argued, how can God, be Infinite Being, if he be not all Beings? And it he be, how can he be One by himself? be a Singular Individual Being, distinct from all others? These were the speculations, that obliged *Spinosa* to conceive of God, that he is the *Ingredient*, Immanent Cause of all Things; and the speculations too, that tempt others, to other mistakes concerning him. But when I come to discourse of the Notions of *Finite* and *Infinite*, and to Represent in what Sense the latter is truly Ascribed to God, I hope to manifest, that there is great *Mistake* in such Speculations and Arguings, and to exempt the true received Notion of Infinity both from these, and from all the like intangling Embarrasments and Difficulties.

The

The *Second* Opinion, is that of Dr. *More* and his Followers, who do hold, that God is an Infinite *Extenſion*; that he is indued indeed with all Goodneſs, Wiſdom, and Power, but he is an Extenſion ſo indued; and of this they are ſo confident, that ſome require a belief thereof as of an Article as great as any in the Creed; an Article that is the Foundation of all Religion; both revealed and Natural. But as I believe, that no Man hath known the Father except the Son, and he to whom the Son hath revealed him, ſo, ſince among all the Revelations that the Son has pleaſed to make of God the Father, this is none [that he is an Extenſion] I cannot admit his being ſo, to be a Notion ſo Eſſential unto all Religion, as they would make it; Eſpecially when I conſider, that it might as eaſily have been ſaid, that God is *Extenſion*, as, that he is a *Spirit*; and Chriſt hath ſaid the latter but not the former. Beſides, I cannot underſtand how Wiſdom, Goodneſs, and Power ſhould be ſaid of meer Extenſion, which is but ſpace; it ſeems to me a leſſer Incongruity (though even this is Incongruity enough) to ſay that God is *Matter* ſo indued, than that he is *Space* ſo indued; ſeeing, even in common ſenſe, there is more of Reality and Being in meer Matter, than

than there is in meer Extenſion or Space. But to urge this Argument more home. By *Extenſion*, (which the perſons who are in this Opinion do Attribute to God,) they muſt mean either *meer* Space, or elſe a *thing* that in the Idea of it is *Spatious*. If meer Space is intended; As this does no ways differ from *inane* or *vacuum*, ſo one may think, it might as well be ſaid (which yet its hard to ſay) that God is an Infinite *inane* or *vacuum*, that is, in plain Engliſh, an Infinite Nothing indued with Wiſdom, Goodneſs and Power, as, that he is infinite Extenſion ſo indued. On the other ſide, if by Extenſion is underſtood a *thing that* in the Idea and firſt Conception of it is Extenſive, that is, a thing that does eſſentially take up ſpace, ſo as that it cannot be conceived, but withal ſpace muſt be Imagined, as an Appurtenant of it ; in this Senſe, I cannot ſee how it differs from *Matter*; and then to ſay, that God is Extenſion, is to ſay, that he is Matter; whereas, God is Pure *Mind*, not *Matter*. *In fine*, as it is certain, that God is Mind, rather than Matter ; ſo likewiſe it is certain, that in the Ideas that we frame of Mind, and of all the things that properly relate to it, ſuch as Wiſdom, Goodneſs, Thought , *&c.* We never do once think of Extenſion or Space;

Space: And if at any time we do endeavour to apply Extenfion or Space unto Mind, or to any thing properly mental, there always arifes a Repugnance in us, upon but the thoughts of it; an Inch, a Foot, a Yard of Underftanding, or Goodnefs, is a *Bull*.

I know it is Argued from the *Omniprefence* of God, that he is Extended; and in truth it is very hard to imagine any prefence with things that are extended, but withal, there muft be an Imagination of fome Extenfion in the thing that is prefent: but ftill, this is but *Imagination*, which is apt to impofe upon us, and therefore it muft be examined by Reafon. And Reafon tells us, that we cannot have a diftinct and clear conception of the *prefence* of God, if we have not (as we have not) fuch an one of his *Effence*, fince the prefence of God is but a Mode of his Effence; and if we have no diftinct and clear Conception of the prefence of God, nor confequently of his Omniprefence, or the way how he is prefent with all his Creatures, where ever they are; I do not fee with what Cogency or Force an Argument can be Deduced from it, in this bufinefs. In fhort, fince things are prefent one with another very *differently*, in proportion to their feveral Natures, it will follow, that
things

things *Mental*, muſt be preſent with others, in much another way than thoſe that are *Material*, and Conſequently that God who is pure Mind, muſt be preſent with Material Beings, much otherwiſe, than theſe themſelves are, one with another. Mind can no more be preſent the ſame way that Matter is, than be the ſame thing with Matter.

CHAP.

CHAP. IV.

Of Mind in Matter.

SECT. I.

Mind as concerned with Matter comes under a double consideration, 1 As it actuates a most subtle and more than Etherial Matter, that is diffus'd throughout the World. 2ly. As it actuates some particular Vechicle or Body. In the first Notion of it, Mind in Matter is the Idea of the Mosaical *Spirit of God This Spirit according to the Scriptural Hypothesis, is the Immediate cause of all things in the first Creation, and ever since. The Being of this Spirit Evinced, both by Authority and by Argument.* Dr. Mores *Distinction, between the Spirit of Nature (which he calls* Principium Hylarchicum) *and the Spirit of God, considered.*

After a Consideration of Mind *as* it is in it self, Pure and *Abstract*, Exempt from all Intrinsecal concernment, and composition with Matter: I come now to consider it as *concerned* with Matter, that is, is, as Acting in, and by means of Matter; in which confideration Mind may be called *second* Mind, as in the former, it may be termed the *first*.

Mind concerned with Matter, may be confidered in *two* refpects, either *as* it has for the Vehicle which it actuates, and by which it acts, all that moft fubtle Matter that does permeate the Univerfe, in the utmoft Extent and Capacity of it; or, *as* it actuates fome particular fyftem of Matter, that may be called a Body, and it is a particular Vehicle.

Mind in the *former* Confideration of it, as it doth actuate, and act in, and by, a moft fubtle matter diffufed throughout the Univerfe, feems to me to be the *Mofaical Spirit* of God, mentioned, *Gen.* 1. *v.* 2. And the *fame* that in the *Scriptural Hypothefis* (which never mentions *Nature* as the Efficient Caufe of any thing, but Reprefents Philofophy only as a *Theology*, that fwallows up the fecond Caufes in Contemplation of the firft,) is the *Caufe* of all productions, the Births, the Growths, and all the Alterations and Changes that come to pafs in the World. This, in that account, is the Principle of Human *Souls, Mal.* 2. 15. *Did he not make one ? Yet had he the Refidue, of the Spirit*: As if he had faid, he wanted not Spirit, [he had more left]

left] to Animate more, had he been pleased to make them, but he made but one; and the Principal too of all *Corporeal Effects*, even of Snow, of Hail, of Ice, of Wind, &c. *Psal.* 147. 15, 16, 17, 18. *He sendeth forth his Commandment upon the Earth, his word runneth very swiftly. He giveth Snow like Wool he scattereth the Hoar Frost like Ashes. He Casteth forth his Ice like Morsels; who can stand before his Cold? He sendeth out his word and melteth them; he causeth his Wind to blow and the Waters Flow.*

To understand this Text with the more clearness, we must have Recourse unto *Genesis*, Ch. 1. *v.* 2, 3, 6, 9, 12, 14, 20, 24, 26. In which we find, in, *v.* 2. mention made of the *Spirit of God* that moved upon the Face of the Waters, as the *Active Principle* that wrought all; and in the 3. and the following verses, of the *Word* or *Commandment* of God, that as a *Directive Principle*, did regulate and order all, so that the Spirit acted accordingly; thus *v.* 3. *God said* let there be *Light*, and there was Light; and *v.* 6. *God said* let there be a *Firmament*, or rather an Expanse, in the midst of the Waters, and it was so, and *v.* 9. *God said,* Let the *Waters under the Heaven be gathered together into one place,* and let the *Dry Land Appear and it was so.*
The

The like in the following works. Now the World in the account of the Holy Scriptures, has the same for its *Conserving*, that it had for its *Procreating* Cause; and therefore as God at first did make All by his Almighty *Spirit* through his *Word*, so the Psalmist tells us, that he still doth; for as at first he said, [*Let there be*] so still, he *Sendeth forth his* [*Commandment,*] and as all was ordered at first by the Divine Word, [He *said*, let there be Light; He *said*, let there be a Firmament, *&c.*] *So still his WORD Runneth very swiftly*: The Spirit of God doth still Execute, as he did at first, all the Directions and Commands are given it; He Produces the Snow; the Hoar Frost; and Ice; he maketh Cold; and Raiseth Winds; and causes all the Alterations that are made in the Air, in the Earth, in a Word, in all the Elements, and in all above them. This is the Scriptural *Hypothesis*; the meaning of which is, that God by his infinite *Wisdom*, as well as *Power*; both *Made* and *Governs*, the World; but to Return.

Of this Spirit, that Penetrates through all the World, and that doth All in it, not only *Moses* has written, but many of the Old *Philosophers*, have also told. *Velleius* in *Cicero*, *l.* 1. *de Nat. Deor.* acquaints

quaints us, concerning *Pythagoras*, *Quod censuit animum esse per Naturam rerum omnem intentum & Commeantem*, that he believed a Mind diffused throughout the whole Nature of things. The same *Velleius* also reports, concerning *Zeno*, that he in some of his Books, discoursed of what he called the *Reason of the Universe*; [*Rationem per omnem pertinentem Naturam.*] In fine, (to omit others) *Plutarch* mentions a *Spirit* that Penetrates throughout the World, [πνεῦμα διῆκον ὅν κόσμε·] And what can this Spirit be, that Penetrates throughout the Universe; that animates it; and is as a common Reason in it (for I will unite the Expressions, and so compleat the Idea;) but the *Mosaical* Spirit?

But not only *Authority* (Sacred and Prophane) evinces, that there is such a *Spirit*, an Energetical Vital Principle, diffused throughout the World; but *Experience* also shows it, if the Experience that we have of such a Principle Diffused throughout *one* Region of it; [our own] may be sufficient to conclude, it is so in *all*; of which Experience I shall speak hereafter, when also the Nature of this Spirit, and the Influence it has upon, and in things, will be set out more clearly, and more fully.

I Know the Learned Dr. *More* hath told us of a *Principium Hylarchicum*; which he defines an *Incorporeal Substance, without Sense and Animadversion, that pervades the Matter of the whole Universe, and exercises in it a Plastical Power according as the Portions of the said Matter are Predisposed*; and this he calls the *Spirit of Nature*, and Distinguishes it from the *Spirit of God*; Affirming, that God doth actuate all the Matter of the Natural Corporeal World by the Spirit of Nature; but that he actually acts in and governs the world of Men and Angels by the Spirit of God. But I have shewed already from the Scriptural *Hypothesis*, that it is *one* Spirit, [the *Mosaical*] that Actuates, and Acts in All, in Men and other Animals, as well as in the World of meer Nature, as to all the operations commonly called Natural; for as to those that are called *Supernatural*, that come from the *Holy Ghost*, or the Comforter, these as they are of another Nature, so the Consideration of them belongs to another place: In fine, the *Principium Hylarchicum*, or Spirit of Nature (as this Learned person calls it,) is but a *Plastick Faculty*, of the *Mosaical* Spirit.

SECT.

SECT. II.

An Inquiry into the Original and Rise of Motion. What is meant by Motion in this Inquiry. That Motion comes from Mind in Matter, or the Mosaical *Spirit. This shewed in many instances, by the Connexion between Cogitation and Motion. How Motion comes from a Principle at Rest, and how Matter from Mind set out in the Metaphysical Hypothesis, and by other Illustrations.*

I Think I shall not step much (if I do at all) out of my way to make Inquiry in this place into the *Original* and Rise of Motion. By *Motion* now I mean not Actual Motion, or Motion as it is the (actual) Translation of Bodies from place to place; which some define [*The Successive Application of a Body in all it hath outwardly, unto the several parts of the Bodies which touch it immediately*;] which is the most usual Sense of the word. But here I mean by it, that *Force*, Energy, or Motive Vertue, called in Latine *Impetus*, from which this Actual Translation, or Successive Application of Bodies does immediately come. And my Enquiry now shall

shall be concerning the *Original* of This, not in *particular* as it is in this or that particular Body, but the Rise of *Impetus* or Motive Force in *general*, which having found, I will *first* remove an Objection, and *then* improve the Discovery, to shew *how* Matter comes from Mind, as well as how Motion doth from a Principle that is at rest.

It must be acknowledged, that there is some appearance (at first sight) of cause to believe, that as *mind* is the first subject of Cogitation, and *matter* the first subject of Extension, so, since *Energy* or Force (the immediate Principle of Action and of Actual motion) is neither Cogitation, nor Extension, that some *third* substance Distinct both from mind and matter, should be the first subject of *it*, and consequently, that there should be *three* Principles, Mind, Matter, and the first Mover. And indeed it looks as if the Scripture *Hypothesis* did countenance *this*; for there mention is made of the *Spirit* which wrought, as the first subject of motion; of the Abyss of *Waters* wrought upon, as the first Recipient Subject; and of the *word* Reason, or Wisdom which directed the Work. But on second Consideration, as it is clear, that all that *Moses* says in his *Genesis*, concerning the Spirit, and the Word, is not

said

said with design to intimate, that really the Spirit was only a meer senseless inartificial Force, or Energy, and that Wisdom or the Word was another distinct Principle, that directed and guided it in all its Motions; but to shew, since we men (in our inadequate way of Conceiving) do distinguish *Wisdom* and *Power*, that all the works of God were made in *Both*, but Both united in one *Demiurgical Mind*, or (to use *Seneca*'s Expression) on *Ratio faciens*. Thus, *Ratio faciens* is the Idea or Notion of the *Mosaical* Spirit, the true *Natura Naturans*, that concurred to make the World, not in the manner that *God* himself did, who, in the Mosaical Hypothesis, Acted only as an External Efficient, but in the way that the *Soul* would do in a living Creature, if first by its Plastic vertue it should form all the members of the Body of it, and afterwards, should inform it, and act in it. And *Cotta* in *Cicero* has as finely as compendiously expressed the Difference between these *two* several ways of working, even in Reference to the World. When L. 3. *de Nat. Deor.* he says, *Ita prorsus existimarem, si illum [mundum] ædificatum, non quemadmodum docebo, à naturâ conformatum putarem.*

It is this Spirit that is the *Original Cause* of the *Impetus*, that is the *nearest cause* of Local

Local Motion; and indeed, it is the Original Cause of all *Mundane Activity* and Energy: Motion comes from Energy or Action, and all Energy and Action from the Mosaical Spirit; [not from meer matter, but from mind in matter.] In short, *Impetus* or Force arises from the *same* Principle that Cogitation or Perception does; as is evident by the following Considerations.

First, The *first mention* that we have of *motion*, or Corporeal Action, is in Relation to the Mosaical Spirit, in *Gen.* 1. 2. where it is said, that the *Spirit of God moved* upon the face of the waters. It is true, the word used in this Text for motion, is seldom used, [but thrice in the whole Scripture, to wit, in this place, in *Deut.* 32. 11. and in *Jer.* 23. 9.] And therefore the direct particular meaning of it will not be easily agreed, but that it imports some motion (which is as much as I do urge it for,) is beyond dispute: *Motum aliquem Notari*, (says Hotting. in Exam. Hist. Creat. Quest. 33.) *non est Dubitandum*.

Secondly, It is farther Evident from the very *Ideas* that we have of things: For we cannot conceive mind as a Perceptive Cogi-

Cogitative substance, but withall, we must conceive it as *Active*, and that there is something *Energetical* in it; whereas, on the other hand, matter may (and in its own proper Idea must) be conceived as a thing that is only *Passive*, not Active; there being nothing of Active or Energetical in it as it is but spacious extensive substance; and therefore Energy and Action cannot be conceived to proceed but from matter, which in its self is Idle and unactive; but rather from mind, which is essentially active and busie.

Thirdly, It may also be argued from the *relation*, that (Experience assures us,) is between Cogitation and Actual motion. For we clearly perceive, that all our voluntary motions do arise from Thought or Imagination; we do move our selves, or any particular part that hath the proper instruments of voluntary motion, and these duly qualified, at our pleasure, when we will; that is, by imagination and thought. We go, we stand still (which is by Tonic motion;) we put our hands, feet, heads, eyes, and other parts of our bodies into motion, and regulate them in their several motions, by will or thought, ay, even cogitation it self in all the several modes of it, as it is sensation, imagination, or ratiocination,

ocination, does ever bear a proportion to some motion; infomuch that as the minute parts of any Organ that ferves unto Cogitation of any kind, are more or lefs in motion; or, (which is meant and is Equivalent,) as the *Organ* is in more or lefs Difpofition and Aptitude to receive impreffions; fo anfwerably, the Act of Cogitation is graduated. Organs that are affected with heavinefs or *torpor*, (as thofe are whofe Particles are too little in motion, and confequently indifpofed for receiving fitting impreffions,) are anfwerably under a *Stupor*, or Diminution of fenfe and perception: but inflamed Organs, whofe particles have too much motion, and confequently are apt to be too *eafily*, or too *much* ftirred, thefe are exquifitely fenfible and tender. In fine, *Reafon* it felf, as to its grounds, is but *Harmony*; a certain modification and turning of the parts, (either the Spirits, or the Filaments,) that are the immediate inftruments of that kind of cogitation; fo that they be not wound up too high, or let down too low; that is, that they be not in too much motion, or aptitude unto it, or in too little, but in a juft mediocrity; and this is to be in *Tune*, or in Harmony. The truth hereof is evident. For if the Organ of Reafon is inflamed, fo that the Particles of it are too

much

much in motion, the action that it exerts in that instance is not reason, but *madness* of one sort or another; and again, if the Organ is torpid, through a defect of motion in the Particles of it, the Cogitation that is exercised in this instance is plain *stupidity* and folly; and the power a dulness or shortness of wit. Wherefore *Aristoxenus* the Musician, who affirmed that the Soul was a Harmony, as he receded not from his Art, so he did not much wander from the true nature of the Soul. In truth, **Harmony** or Proportion is the *Soul of the World.* For if we look well, we shall find that, that which formalizes things, and qualities, and which makes them be of this or that kind, and to act in this or that way, is nothing but the Proportion or *Logos* that is in them; that is, it is the *Tuning* of them in the world, and one to another, as to parts, and motions: most, if not all the *Specifical Qualities* and Operations that are in the World, arise from hence; which are therefore called *Occult*, because this Spring and Original of them is so little regarded; but of this more in another, and perhaps a more proper place,

But to more illustrate the former Argument, and show in a fuller light, the relation

tion between Cogitation and actual motion; I will enter farther into the Consideration of *motion*; and will manifest, both the *subtlety* of it, and also the *Correspondence* which it holds with Mind, or the *Perceptive*. I will not speak now of the motion that is *Local* to such a Degree, that it falls under *Observation* of the sense, but of *that* motion (for motion it is) that contributes to the *being* of sense; which for Distinction sake may be called *Impression*. We are convinced by sense, that in the *Impressions* that make it, there is a great deal of subtlety, and this too in various *Degrees*; and we are equally convinced, that there are various sensitive *Powers* to receive *them*, in those several Degrees. Thus the impression made upon the *Eye*, that causes *Vision*, is by many Degrees more delicate and fine than that which causes the *Feeling*; since the Object seen by the Eye, and Consequently making a Visive impression (upon it) ordinarily doth not make any upon the sense of feeling. I say ordinarily, because sometimes, where the impression of the visible is very strong, as when one looks upon the Sun, or on some other very strong and vigorous Light, the *feeling* of the *Eye* is affected, as well as the *Sight*, so that there is a sense of *pain*, from a solution of Continuity. Which plainly evinces

evinces (to note it by the by) that all visible impression, tho' it be not sensibly a motion, yet really is so, since even visible impressions, if strong and vigorous, are painful; and consequently, are motions; for nothing causes pain but motion; pain being nothing but little Spasms and Tensions of the parts; and if strong impressions be motions, weaker ones are so too; tho' in a less degree.

Again, The impression made upon the *Ear*, that causes *sound*, tho' it be by much a less fine and delicate one than that upon the Eye, which causes Light or Colour, it is however of far greater fineness and delicacy than that Impression which produces *pain* in the Ear; For as we *see* without pain, so, ordinarily we *hear* without it; that is, we are affected by sonorous Objects, which do propagate their motions to our ears, with the sentiment of sound, without being sensible of this Affection any other way. And yet if the sound be too intense, it always *pains*, and often breaks, or too much stretches the *Timpanum* or Drum of the Ear. The observation that some Philosophers have taken of this latter effect, occasion'd them to make a *Maxim*, that *an Excellent Object destroys the Sense*; but possibly this must be understood with Correction, not so much in respect

spect of the Faculty or Perceptive *Power*, as of the *Organ*; for could the Organ bear those stronger impressions, without Alteration or Hurt, the perceptive Faculty would not be offended; it is not the sentiment, either that of *Light*, or that of *Sound*, that offends, but the motion that causes *it*, which is too strong for the Organ, and dissolves or alters its Texture. In fine, the impression that causes *Intellection*, is by much a finer and more subtle one, than that which causes sensation, whether External, or Internal; and that by as many degrees as *Intellectual Ideas* are more fine and subtle than *Images*, and the *Understanding* a finer and more delicate Faculty than the *Sense*.

By *Finer* and Delicater *Impressions*, I mean such as have less of Local Motion. By Finer and Delicater *Faculties*, I mean such as are sensible of Finer and Delicater Touches, or Impressions.

In this sense, the *Imagination* must needs be a finer and more delicate faculty than any external sense, for as much as it receives the impressions of External Objects but by *Reflection*, or Communication from the *Sensories*, but these have them *directly* from the very *Objects* themselves; and by the same Reason, the *Understanding*, that receives impressions from the *internal sense*,

must

muſt needs be (as indeed it is) a much finer and delicater faculty than *That*.

Upon the whole, it is evident, that there is a near relation between actual motion and cogitation, and conſequently, that it is no unreaſonable thought to think, that as they are *near of kin*, ſo both are Off-ſprings of *one* Original cauſe, [mind in matter;] but then it will follow alſo, that motion, and indeed all Energy whatever in the Spring and Principle of it is *Reſt*, for ſo mind is. But this is the difficulty. For that motion ſhould come from a Principle that is at reſt, appears as unintelligible, as that Froſt ſhould come from Fire, or Darkneſs from Light.

Wherefore to make this clear, I muſt conſider things in the *Metaphyſical Hypotheſis*, as all are underſtood to come from one, by way of *Emanation*: and thus, all *Created Being* is compared to *Light*, that flows from the Sun; and then its *Emanation* is in the ſame manner, as the *Radiation* of Light, which is from a Center into an Orb or Sphere, in *Extenuating* Lines. Now in this Hypotheſis, as all Beings (even thoſe that are moſt oppoſite) do come from *one*, ſo they come from *it* in this way, that the more *Removed* any is from the *Central* Being, the more *Extenuated* it is; that is, as *God* or pure mind is the Central Being,

that

that *Sun*, that is the Father of Lights; so all the Being that proceeds from *him*, has less of Light and more of Darkness, in proportion to the distance it has, upon the Scale of Being, and in its utmost *Elongation* or Removal from him, terminates in that, which in Appearance has nothing of Resemblance to the Original Light; but (to be compared with it) is only *Darkness* and shadow; and this last is the Idea of *meer matter*, as that of the Central Light is of pure Mind. God is Light; Matter is *Darkness*; all intermediate Beings are *Light* and *Darkness*, in several proportions.

What I have said is sensibly set out in the *shades* of Colours, and in *Colours* themselves, which are but shades of *Light*; For the Extremes of *any* Colour, for Example, the *Brightest* Red, and the *Darkest*; or the Extreams of *all* Colours, as *White* and *Black*; compare them each with other, and they are so contrary, that nothing can be more, especially the two latter; and yet they do participate, the former not only of Colour in general, but also of Red; and the latter, tho' of no particular Colour, yet of Light, which is the Ground of Colour in general; and also the Darkest Red, if it doth not come from the Brightest; and the Blackest Colour

lour from the Whitest; yet, by the Gradation of Shades, or Participle, intermediate Colours, they are so continued one to another, that the Ascent and Descent from one unto the other is most Agreeable and Delightful, as made by easie steps, without any Patches, or Chasms. It is true, if we look on Contraries in their *Physical* Consideration, so they are of *opposite Natures*, opposite Operations, and one expels the other, when they are immediately set together; but if we look upon them in their *Metaphysical* Consideration, so they are but *degrees* of the same nature, and capable of being United and Reconciled; insomuch, that One in a right sense may be said to come from Another; as Darkness from Light. For however contrary *Light* and *Darkness* are, each unto other, as to Qualities and Physical Operation, and so in their Physical Consideration, yet as to their Metaphysical, they differ but in *degrees*; both have the same grounds; for Shadow really is but lesser Light, occasion'd by the interposition of an Opaque Body, and Darkness is but a great Shadow. And thus a *Flat* and a *Sharp*, tho' contrary sounds, as to their *Physical* Consideration, yet as to their *metaphysical*, they are but different degrees; the Sharp a greater, the Flat a lesser degree

gree of Celerity. And thus as Darkness comes from Light, only by the Lessning or Extenuating of it; so may matter come from mind: *mind* is pure Light, or, all Being in Eminence; but *matter*, as it doth Participate nothing at all of mind, but only by meer Existence, so it is meer darkness, without the least degree of Vitality or Life; and *all Beings* between Mind and Matter, are as *Colours*, in respect of Light, or as *Shades*, in respect of any particular Colour.

But to add some further cleering to this Subject, and to shew how actual local motion may come from a Principle that is at rest, which being shewed, will shew withall *how* Matter may come from mind, since there is no greater Repugnance (even to common sense) in the one, than is in the other, I will consider the Relation that the *Center* of a Circle has unto its *Circumference*, and how things are in the *one*, and how in the *other*; For this will afford it much Illustration. In the *Center* then of a Circle, or of a moved Sphere, all is at Rest, and out of *it* all in motion, but in such proportion, that that portion of a *Radius* which is at a farther distance from the Center, is *more* in motion, by reason of that distance, and that which is nearer

is

is *less*; which is evident even to sense, in the following Diagram.

In the three Concentrical Circles, *B. C. D. E. F G.* if the Ray *A. B. D. F.* is supposed to be moved from *F.* to *G.* it will appear to any that considers, that in the same time that in the inmost Circle it doth move from *B.* to *C.* and in the middle from *D.* to *E* it moves in the outmost from *F.* to *G.* that is, it moves faster, and is more in motion, the farther it is from the Center *A.* and only because it is so. Again, on the Contrary, in the same time that the *Radius* moves in the outmost Circle from *F.* to *G.* it moves in the middle but from *D.* to *E.* and in the inmost (which is nearest to the Center *A.*) but from *B.* to *C.* that is, it has more of Rest, and less of Motion, the nearer it is to the Center, and in the Center has no motion at all, but is at pure rest. Even sense acquaints us, that the Arch or Space *F. G.* is much Greater than the Space *D. E.* and that *D. E.* is Greater than *B. C.* and so on the contrary, that the Arch or Space *B. C.* is less by much than *D. E.* and *D. E.* (by much) than the Arch or Space. *F. G.* and yet all the Spaces are supposed to be passed by the Ray *A. B. D. F.* in the same time.

time. Now that which paſſes a greater ſpace in the ſame time, is more in motion, and has greater Celerity; and that which paſſes a leſs, is leſs in motion, and has leſs of Celerity; and therefore ſince the nearer the Ray is unto the Center, the leſs ſpace it paſſes in the ſame time, and the farther off it is, the more it paſſes, and that more or leſs as it is farther off, or nearer; it evidently follows, that farther off from the Center, a Ray has more of motion, and as it is nearer to it, it has leſs, and in the Center has none.

[145]

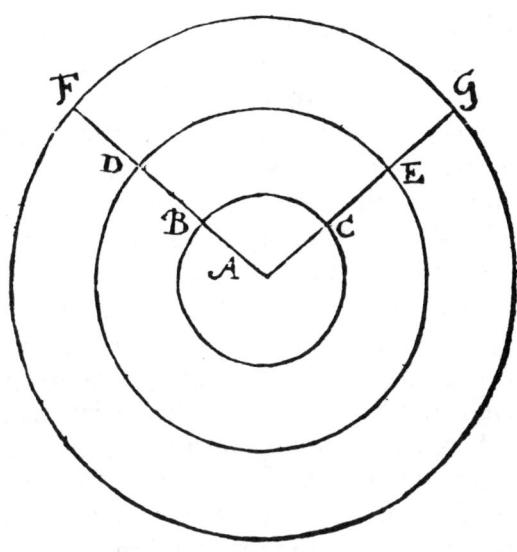

Well then, supposing that the Principle of Energy and Motion is in the *Center* of the Orb of Being, (and we may well suppose it, since even *Nature* has its Sphere of Activity, and Acts as from a Center to a Circumference; (so *Seeds* Act, so *Light* Acts and Diffuses itself;) it is certain that motion must come from something not in Motion, but at Rest; for so that is, which is in the Center; and indeed, else there must be infinite progression in Motions. *Again*, since in the Orb of being, Pure Mind is in the Center,

L   and

and matter in the utmoſt Circumference, it follows, that the nearer things are unto pure mind, and the more they do participate of that, the more they have of Reſt, and the leſs of motion; but the farther off they are from pure Mind, and the nearer to matter, the more in motion they are. And indeed, all Energy in matter is Local Motion. Thus all the Effects of *Mechaniſm*, as they are purely material, ſo they are performed *only* by Local Motion; but the buſineſs of Cogitation, even in the loweſt ſtep of it, which is ſenſation, as it is of nearer Relation unto mind than to matter, ſo it is performed rather by way of mutation, than of Local motion; the *Eye* is not ſenſible of any motion imparted to it, nor is the Ear, or the Noſe, or any other of our Senſories, and yet each is ſenſible of a mutation made therein, (or rather in the Faculty) which comes from motion. But tho' the more refined any Beings are, and the nearer that they are to the Central Mind, the more at reſt they be, and the leſs in motion in their ſeveral Actions; and conſequently Abſtract Spirits that do not live in groſs Elementary Bodies, are more at reſt, and have leſs of motion, in the exerciſes of their ſeveral Powers, than Men have, who are imbodied in Elementary Vehicles;

cles; yet *no Spirit* whatsoever but only *God* himself, who only is Pure Mind, is *so* wholly, so Absolutely at Rest, *as* that it sees all Things at once, by one Entire view and Intuition; all Principles and all Conclusions in them; all Ends and all Means and Motives to them; without the least degree of Succession, or any Addition. Only the *Central Being* sees *so*, and he doe's.

For seeing all the Circumference is in the Center, so that all the Lines however divided they be in the former, do meet together in the latter; it is plain, that an Eye placed in the *Center*, must needs see all in the *Circle*, as clearly as any thing in it; and this too with one Individual, single Intuition, without Succession, or, Addition; seeing there is nothing of Motion, but all is Rest in the Center. And this properly is to *see in Eternity*. Thus *God* sees. But all *other Beings* beside God, *as* they are not God, or Pure mind, *so* they are not in the Center, and not being the Center, but at Distance from it, some at Greater, some at Lesser, but All at some, they All have something of Motion, and consequently cannot Act, or See, in the same manner as Central Pure Mind, by way of Absolute Rest, without Succession, or Addition,

and

and without Distinction of past, present, and to come: For tho' all the Lines do meet in the Center, yet there being no place without it in which they do so, Creatures cannot see as God sees, no more than they can be in the Center as God is. It is too short and Inadequate a way of Arguing to Infer that any Creatures can see All things at once, but from the notions (confused enough) that we Mortals have of *Time* and *Eternity*; as that *Time* is Successive, *Eternity* a Permanent Duration; together with a Conceit, that *all Spirits* (they being things Abstract and Separate from Bodies,) both Are, and Act, *in Eternity*, as all Imbodied Beings Are, and do Act, in *Time*. Certainly every Being but God, is in Time, tho' not in the same Kind of Time; for as God only is in *the Center*, so he only is Absolutely *in Eternity*. And if Time is taken for all Duration that is not Eternity, God only is without Time, and so without Succession of Actions. But to Return.

SECT.

SECT. III.

Of Mind as it Actuates a certain Particular Body; Mind in this Notion called a Soul. Body is a System of Organs. Soul and Body an Animal. Body Considered two ways. To wit, in Reference to External Objects, and in Reference to the Internal Principle that Acts it. In the First Consideration of Body, the Ends and uses of Organs are shewed, and withal the Reason of their variety. This Illustrated by several Instances and Observations. The use of Body in Relation to the Internal Principle that Actuates it, is to Individuate and Singularize that Principle. This set out in sensible and plain Resemblances. A Comparison between Vital and Locomotive Energy; with a Recapitulation of the whole Discourse, as it unfolds the Mystery of Animals.

WE have Considered Mind in the first Step of Relation that it carries unto Matter, Namely, as it doe's *Actuate a most subtle Matter diffused throughout the Universe,* in which Notion it is called *Spirit* simply, as was shewed from *Malachy*, *Ch.* 2. *v.* 15. Come we now to Consider it it in the next place, as it *Actuates some Particular System of Matter*, in a Particular Manner; and so it is called a *Soul*; and that Particular System of Matter, which it doth Actuate, is a *Body*, or a Particular Vehicle; and the Result of both an *Animal*. An *Animal* is nothing but Soul and Body together; or a Body Actuated by a Soul. A *Body* is a System of Organs; an *Organ* is Matter framed and Contrived after a Particular Manner for some Animal Use, and End; some Use, End, or Action of a Soul: A *Soul* is a certain Determinate Vital Energy; or a certain Portion of the Spirit of the Universe, Vested in a Body, or particular Vehicle; in which Notion all *Souls* are *Spirits*; as indeed they are stiled in the Holy Scripture, wherein we Read of the Spirit of the *Beast*, tho' it goes Downward, as well as of the Spirit of a *Man* that goes Upward.

This Discourse I fear will seem a little Mysterious; and therefore to Inlighten it, and withal to open (tho' but in general) the Mystery of the *Animal Nature*, and, by Analogy unto it, the Nature of *other Vivents*, I will Resume it from the Beginning, and speak more Distinctly: taking my Rise from *Bodies*, or Systems of Organs, which coming under Sense, are better

better known unto us than Spirits or Souls.

Body then, as it is a Syſtem of Organs, has a *Double* Relation, and ſo may be Conſidered two ways; either with Reſpect to External *Objects* by which it ſelf is Affected, and by means thereof, the Mind; or elſe with Reſpect to the Internal *Principle* that doth Inform and Actuate it, and Act in it, which Principle it doth *Individuate* and Singularize.

We will firſt Conſider a Body in the Relation that it has unto *External Objects*, and here we muſt ſet out the *Nature*, that is, the Ends and Uſes of the Organs which compoſe a Body, as alſo the Reaſon of the *Variety*, and number of thoſe Organs; why *any* Organs at all, and why *many*: both which will be done with one Performance. An Organ properly, is Matter Particularly Textured, and Framed for ſome Particular uſe: And an Animal Organ is Particularly Textured, and Framed for an Animal uſe: I will give the Example in only Senſitive Animals, and in the Acts of Senſation, as being beſt underſtood; but what is ſaid of Senſation, and of the Organs of it, will, by Proportion, hold in all the other Actions of Animals, and in all other Organs, with a due Alteration.

In all *Acts of Sensation* there is first an *Affection* of the Organ, and then a *Perception* of that Affection by the Soul; or rather, a Perception Excited in the *Soul* by means of that Affection; and this is the *End* of the *Organ*, and the only Use of it, that the Soul makes, to wit, to come by means thereof unto a Perception of External Objects; as, to see their Colours, to hear their Sounds, to Relish the several Tasts they have, and the like. In short, a Soul cannot but by the *means of Organs*, take any notice of External Objects, nor the Organ be a means of conveying any notice to the Soul, but by being first *Affected* it self. Now the *Affection* of the Organ arises from a *Perception* (may I so express it) or a Reception of the *Motions* Communicated to it by Objects; and a *Capacity* for this Reception from the Particular *Frame* of the Organ. For since all Matter indifferently is not capable of receiving all kinds of Motions and Impressions; but that for some *Particular Motions* and Impressions (of which sort are sensible ones) there must be *Particular Textures* and Frames of Matter to *Catch* them; it follows, that there must be *Organs*; and these too in such *Variety* and Number: there must be *Organs*, to Receive the Impression and Motions of Objects, which

without

without a Particular Texture of Matter could not be Received ; and there muſt be *Variety* of Organs, to Correſpond theſe various Kinds of Motions and Impreſſions that are in Coloured, in Sonorous, in Sapid, and in other *Species* of Objects.

This will be better conceived in ſome Inſtances, by which it ſhall be made appear, that for the Reception of certain Particular Motions, there muſt be certain *Particular Textures*, and Diſpoſitions of Matter ; ſo that Matter in ſome certain Frames and Diſpoſitions of it will *Catch*, and be Affected with, ſome certain Particular Motions, that in others, it will not be *Touched* with It is Generally Obſerved, that an *Uniſon* ſtring will Receive the Motion, and ſo, Tremble, when another alſo Uniſon is made to Sound, and yet all other Strings of the ſame Inſtrument, that are not Uniſons, ſhall remain inſenſible and unmov'd. *Cardan* Obſerved, that in a certain Church, in which were ſeveral Images of Wax, but one would move and Tremble, and one always would, at the Ringing of a Sacring Bell. Mr. *Boile* has taken notice of the like Mechanical Perception, in ſeveral Empty Drinking-Glaſſes of Fine white Metal ; he ſays, that cauſing the Strings of a Muſical Inſtrument to be variouſly ſcrewed

screwed up, and let down, and briskly struck, he observed, that the Motion of one String, when it was stretched to a certain *Note*, or Tone, would make one of the Glasses Ring, and not the other; nor would the sound of the same String Tuned to another Note, sensibly Affect the same Glass; tho' perhaps, says he, it might have its Operation upon another. In fine, there are *Tonical Echo's*, that Return not the Voice but when it has some Peculiar Musical Note, and then it doe's. Thus Organs are Matter Particularly Textur'd, to the End to make them capable of Receiving some Particular Motions: so that a *Sensitive Organ* may be Defined, a System of Matter Particularly Framed, Disposed, and Textured for receiving some Particular Motion of External Bodies, and for Conveying it to the Soul.

So much concerning Body in its Relation to External *Objects*; come I now to consider it in the Relation which it has to the *Soul*, (the Internal Principle that Actuates it, and Acts in, and by it;) and so, the Great work and Business of the Body is to *Singularize* and Individuate the *General Vital Principle* of the Universe, that it may become a *Soul*, or a Particular Vital Principle of a certain Particular Body. To understand this it must be Consider'd,

Consider'd, that the *Mosaical Spirit* (the Rise and Principle of all Created Cogitation,) as it is Extended throughout the whole Universe; so, to become in Particular a *Soul*, of any Particular *Animal*, it must be *Singularized*, and Individuated, that is, it must be *Apportioned* (as it were) to that Particular Animal, which it comes *to be* by means of the Body. To Illustrate this, it must be Remembred, that a *Voice* or Sound Diffused throughout the whole capacity of the *Medium* (as the *Mosaical* Spirit is throughout that of the universe) is yet in the *Phonocamptick Center* or object (which is nothing but a place conveniently Disposed for this Purpose,) *so Individuated* and Singularized (as the Mosaical Spirit is supposed to be by a Congruous fit Body,) that Really it has *other Affections* and Properties, than *those* it owns, in all the rest of the *Medium*, insomuch that by Vertue of it, this *place* instead of being a *Medium* of Sound, becomes to all Appearance a *Principle* of it, and so a *Speaker*, and this is called an *Echo*. It may also be set out in a *Speculum* or Looking-Glass, (for a Body is to the Mosaical Spirit, what a *Speculum* or Looking-Glass is to the Image of an Object in the *Medium*;) A *Speculum* Catches the Diffused Image, and *so Singularizes* it, that

it

it becomes a very Different thing, and puts on other very Different Properties than those it has in the *Medium*, for in the *Looking-Glass* it doth appear as an Object which it doe's not out of it. But what doe's set it out most naturally, is, that it is so in *Man*; For the Soul or Cogitative Principle of a Man, as it is Extendded throughout the whole Capacity of the Body, in like manner as the *Mosaical* Spirit is, throughout that of the Universe; so it is *Singularized* and Individuated, in, and by, the particular *Organs*: insomuch that the *Eye* only does *See*; the *Ear* only does *Hear*, and only the *Tongue Tasts*, in Vertue thereof; for which Reason these are owned to have several particular *Faculties*, which are as so many several Souls unto them. Now what the Organs are to the Soul in any Body (that is but a System of Organs,) Bodies themselves are, unto the *Mosaical* Spirit, the great Soul of the Universe, of which all particular Bodies are Organs. But since this Notion is of so much Importance, that it will deserve a more particular Consideration, and I design to give it one in another Chapter, I shall dismiss it at present, without further Insisting on it; and now will only add some *Improvement* to the former Discourse, by making a *Comparison* between

tween the Vital and the Mechanical Energy.

First then I lay it down as certain, that there is such a thing as a *Vital*, as well as a *Mechanical* Energy: by *Vital Energy* I mean all that is not meerly Mechanical; and therefore do comprehend in that Term whatever is properly *Mental*; by *Mechanical Energy* I mean Impulse or Springines, the nearest Physical Principle of Actual Local Motion. Now we are as sure by our senses, and by the Reflection that we make upon our selves, and upon the Notices which we receive from Things without us, that there is such a thing as a *Vital* Energy, as we are that there is a *Mechanical*: Because we are as much assured of the Effects of the *one*, as we are of those of the *other*; as much assured that there is Life, Sensation, and Intellection, that come from a Vital; as we are that there are Actual Local Motions; Motions of Ascent and Descent, Motions Direct, and Motions Circular, *&c* which (as Motions) come from Impulse, the Mechanical Energy.

Again; As it is Certain that *Local Motion*, or that Impulse which is the nearest Physical Principle of it, is *not* Matter, or Materiate, but yet is *in* Matter, as United unto it: so by this Consideration we may
become

become as certain, that *Vital Energy* and the Effects of it, *though* they be Immaterial, *yet* they may be in Matter; since there needs no more of Hooks and Crooks to make the Latter, than to make the Former to stick, and hold together.

In the next place; As the Mechanical, or Loco-motive Energy is Diffused *throughout the World* (for there is nothing in this, that is Entirely at Rest;) so is the Vital: Since it is certain that wherever, and whenever, any Matter becomes Disposed, the Vital Principle is *always at hand* to Actuate that Matter, and Act in it, according as the Dispositions of it do Invite or Permit: All *Putrefaction* or Digestion *any where*, determines in *Insects*, or little Animals, (as Experience evinces,) the Spirits being Unfettered and let Loose thereby.

And yet *as* the Mechanick or Loco-motive Impulse is not Received in all Textures of Matter indifferently, but that, (as I have showed already) there must for some certain Modifications of Local Motion, be certain particular Textures of Matter, *so* neither is the Vital Energy Catcht and Received indifferently by all Textures of Matter; but as all Life consists in Motion, or in something Analogous, so for certain Gradations and Exercises of Life,

Life, there muſt be cerain particular Fabricks and Textures of Matter, called *Organs,* and alſo certain particular Diſpoſitions in the *Mechanical Spirits* (for ſo I call the ſubtle Active Corpuſcles in every Concrete) that are the immediate inſtruments of the Vital Principle in all its Actions of Life, in this Corporeal World.

So that as Actual Motion, the Effect of Loco-motive Energy, and even Loco-motive Energy it ſelf (as taken for Impulſe) is not Material in this Senſe, that it does *conſiſt* of Matter, yet, if to be material be underſtood of that which is *Dependent on* Matter, and ſo Dependent that it cannot be without it; in the Senſe of the word, not only actual Motion, but even *Impulſe* (the neareſt Phyſical principle of Motion) is material, ſince neither of them can be but in, and by the means of Matter. In like manner, the Vital Principle that Animates Corporeal Beings, though it is not material in this Senſe, that it is *only* Matter, or a mode of Matter, yet in another it is, that it *ſo Depends* in all its Animal Operations, that it cannot exerciſe any but by means of Mater, and according to the Texture and Quality of it. Nothing can be plainer than this is to Senſe, for in all the Acts of Perception, not only the ſenſitive, but the Intellectual, *as* the Organs are,

are, fo are the Actions; if the Organs are found and duly Difpofed, the Actions are Conformable; but if the Organs are out of Tune and Vitiated, the Actions are fo likewife; Ay, are Totally Abolifhed, if the Organs are fpoiled; Befides, the feveral Kinds, and Degrees, of Deliration, that men themfelves are Subject unto, accordingly as their Spirits are ill Qualified and Diftempered, do further Confirm it.

Upon the whole, as the Vital Energy it Diffufed (as Light is) throughout the Univerfe; fo according to the feveral Textures of Matter that do catch it, as a *Speculum* does the Light, it Exerts it felf; and being Catcht and Retained by the *Congruity* of the Body, (for it is Congruity only, not Hooks or Crooks, that holds them together,) it is called a *Soul*, and the whole Complex, [of Body and Soul] an *Animal*.

What I have faid, does more particularly regard the *Animals*, I call *Vifible*, which we are better Acquainted with, than with *others of a Higher Nature*; but yet, with a very eafie Application, and by way of Analogy, it will alfo open the Nature of *thefe*: However, this Admonition doth Remind me of the next Head to which I muft pafs, and that is, the *Diftribution* of Animals.

CHAP.

CHAP. VII.

Animals are either Invisible or Visible; in the Former sort I reckon Angels, Good and Bad, which are Etherial: As also the Genii, which are Aerial Animals. Invisible Animals, why called Spirits. That there are Spirits Evinced, 1. From the general Tradition of the World. Mr. Hobbs's Evasion of this Argument Considered. 2. From Operations that cannot be Accounted for but from such Causes. 3. From Intelligences and Notifications that cannot be Resolved but upon this Hypothesis. 4. From Spectra or Apparitions. Of the way and manner how Spirits do Appear, that it is twofold, Real and Visional. That Good Angels when they do Appear are called πνεύματα or Spirits; and the Bad φαντάσματα or Fantomes.

SECT. II.

I Have spoken of Animals in General, but to bring a greater Light toward the Understanding of the Animal Nature, I must consider its *Distribution*, and show the General Kinds or sorts of Animals that are in the Universe. And Animals in Conformity unto the Bodies that do help to compose them, are either *Visible*, or *Invisible*. By *Visible* Animals, I mean such as do consist of gross matter, and so have Bodies that naturally come under the perception of the external sense; by *Invisible* Animals, I mean such as have Bodies so refined, that naturally they come not under the perception of *All*, or *Any* of the External Senses.

Visible Animals, which are the Animals that compose this *Lower Elementary World*, (for I will not undertake to speak of any such as may be in the other, commonly called the Superiour and Celestial,) the farther Discourse of them is properly referred unto *Physicks*, and therefore I shall enter no farther thereinto at this time, but proceed to treat of the *Invisible*.

By Invisible Animals, I mean Angels, good and bad, which I call Ætherial Animals, as also those Æreal ones (some Ludicrous, some Torvous) that are called *Genii*; all which, with the several kinds they farther branch into, I will comprehend under one name [of *Spirits*,] and so speak something of their *Nature*; Demonstrate their *Reality* and Existence; and
in

in fine, add something concerning their *Apparition*, and the *ways* of it.

As to their *Nature* in General, I think I shall have said all is necessary for me to say at this time, when I shall have shewed, that there is a sense in which it may be truly said, they are *Incorporeal*, (as said they are, generally;) and yet there is a sense too, in which, they must be acknowledged to be *Corporeal*, if the having *any* mixture of matter in their Composition can suffice (as I know it will be yielded me it doth) to make them properly denominated *such*.

The sense in which Spirits are truly said to be *Incorporeal*, will be best understood by shewing the reason how the Attribute of being *Corporeal* becomes *Appropriated* unto visible Animals; to comprehend which, we must consider, that in order to our conversing with Objects, and taking Cognizance of them, we are endowed with *two* sorts of Faculties, the **Sense**, and the **Understanding**; and that the **Sense** (even to Sense) is an *Organical Material* Power, for we do see the Organs it uses, the Eye for Seeing, the Ear for Hearing, and the like for all the rest; but that the **Understanding** is (to *Sense*) an *Inorganical Immaterial* Power, there not *Appearing* any *Sensible Organ*, by means of which,

which, it does exert or put forth its Acts. Now in conformity to this *Distinction* between our Faculties, we do make *one* of their Objects, (nor can we do it more agreeably:) calling the Substances that do properly come under the notice and observation of our sense, *Bodies*; and those that do not, but are only inferred and perceived by the understanding, *Spirits*: the former are corporeal material Substances; because perceived by *sense*, which is a material Organical Power; but the latter, such as Angels and other Spirits, are said to be immaterial, incorporeal, because we *cannot* See, or Feel, or Tast, or Smell them in their own Subsistences: In a word, we cannot perceive them in their own proper beings by any of the *Senses* we have, but only by the Ratiocination and Discourse of the *Understanding*, which (to sense) is an Inorganical Immaterial Power. And our Saviour Christ, when after his Resurrection, he appeared to his Disciples, and they apprehended that they had seen a Vision, to convince them of the Reality of his *Corporeal* Existence, and that he was not a Spirit, or an Apparition only, as they took him to be, he Appeals unto their *Sense*, and particularly to that of *Touch*, *Luke* 24. 39. Behold, says he, *my Hands, and my Feet, that it is I my self,*

self, for a Spirit hath no Flesh and Bones as you see me have: Wherein he goes upon these Notions, that a *Spirit* is an invisible Thing, a Thing that in its own reality cannot be seen, nor be felt, but only be understood; and that, that substance which comes under the notice and cognisance of the sense is a *Body*.

And in this sense of the word [Body] all Spirits are really un-imbodied incorporeal things; they have not *such* Bodies of Flesh and Bone, or Organs that come under the Observation and notices of *sense*, as we have; but in another sense of the word, as Body is not taken restrainedly, for that only which is *sensible*, but more largely, for *any System of Matter* whatever, (whether so refined and subtle that it comes not within the compass of any external sense, or so gross, that it may be perceived by it;) so Spirits are Corporeal and Embodied: That is, they are material (as well as mental) Beings; minds indeed they are, but Minds *in Matter*, or Animals. In this, *Scaliger* consents with me, who in his Exercitations (*Exerc.* 307. §. 38.) boldly says, *Spiritus Latinis & Græcis Omnibus, Philosophis, Medicis Oratoribus, Corpus est: id est, Materia, & Forma.*

This will be Evident, if we consider (1.) That Absolute Purity, or Exemption

from

from *all* Matter, is the peculiar *Prerogative of God*, who only is Pure Light, without any mixture of Darkness; it is only *he*, the Central Being, (he that is absolute pure being) that is pure unmixed mind; all other beings but *he* must be impure, and have some ingredience of *matter* in their Composition; without *which*, as they would be pure Mind, so (being pure mind) they would be God. Secondly, Were all or any Spirits, except the infinite Almighty *Center* and Spring of All Absolutely pure, without any mixture of Matter; absolutely simple, without any Real Composition; there could be no *Distinction* among them, either in Respect of *Kinds*, or of *Individuals*; since *Alterity* (and where there is Distinction, there must be Alterity; *unus & alius, est alter & alter,*) cannot consist with *Absolute simplicity*; Composition is *Unity*, but simplicity is *Unicity*.

To be more Particular; were Spirits Absolutely Pure and Simple, without any Admission of Matter, there could be no Distinction among them in respect of *Kinds*. For what should difference them? if there were nothing in them but that, wherein they did all agree; as there would be nothing else but that, if all of them were pure and simple: Things that *Differ* in in something, and withal in something *Agree*, cannot be *Pure* or *Simple*: for all have something that is *Common*, in which they do agree, and all something *not* Common, in which they differ; it is plain, that each of them Consists of Thing, and Thing; and Things that Consist of Thing and Thing are Compounded; not Pure and Simple Things.

Again, were Spirits absolutely pure and simple, without any Concretion of Matter, there could be no distinction among them as to *Individuals*, as well as none in relation to Kinds. For since all Individuation (except only that of the Central pure mind) is *Numerication*, and all Numerication arises from Division, and Division has no place but in Matter, or in Things by means of matter: It is evident that there can be no distinction of Spirits as to Individuation, if there be no ingredience of matter in their making. Things are said to differ *in number*, (and so all Individuals differ, as well those of one and the same, as those of divers *Species*,) that however identified they be in other Respects, yet do so differ, that one is not the other; which cannot be without Division, of one from the other; nor Division be without matter: *Unum* is not only *Indivisum in se*, but *Divisum à Quolibet alio*. As for *Metaphysical*

physical Matter and Metaphysical *Form*, or that distinction that some make of (substantial) *Power* and *Act*, they are but *meer Words*, without any signification (at least in my understanding) if they are not reduced to *Matter* and *Mind*; which are the *only* Metaphysical Principles of Things, that are *Existent* and Real. In short, we may observe *in our selves*, (that Mind as I have noted before) is *Individuated by Matter*, since even sense is seeing in the *Eye*; Hearing in the *Ear*; Tasting in the *Tongue*, &c.

Another Consideration that Induces me to believe, that all Spirits are *Animals*, and vitally united unto Matter, of one sort or another, is, that the Apostle *Paul*, in a Discourse of his Concerning the Resurrection, 1 *Cor.* 15. doe's Speak of a *Spiritual* Body, in Contradiction to a *Natural*, as of the Body that All that do Arise in Christ shall be Cloathed withal; and Christ himself tells us, that All that shall Attain that glorious Resurrection, shall be ἰσάγγελοι, as Angels; to wit, in Respect of their Spiritual Bodies, that shall Invest them: and if Glorified Men shall be *as* Angels, Angels must be *as* Glorified Men; that is, they must have Bodies, tho' Glorious and Spiritual Bodies.

In

In fine, that Spirits are *Incorporeal* Beings in this fenfe, that they have not fuch Grofs Elementary Bodies as we have, of Flefh and Blood and Bones, doe's not Infer, that they are *fo* in every fenfe of that word; efpecially if we Confider, that (as the Apoftle affures us) there may be *Spiritual Bodies*; and there Appears not any Incoherence (in this,) that Spirits fhould have Spiritual Bodies. Befides, the Underftanding it felf, that, unto fenfe, is an *Inorganical* Immaterial Faculty, is not Abfolutely *fo*, but has the *Animal Spirits* for an Organ, fince as thefe are Difpofed and Textured, well or ill, even fo the Exercifes of that noble power, are either right, or depraved; and from the differences in *thefe* Spirits do come the differences of *Wits*, which are many. Ay, poffibly thofe Animal Spirits (or fomething that refembles them) may compofe the *Body* which accompanies the departing Soul: for that fome kind of Body does, which in the *Greek* is called αὐγόαδες, the Learned *Origen* has told us, *L. 2. Contra Celfum*: which *Body* he alfo fays, is *that*, the Separated Soul is ufed to appear in; but as to this, I fhall offer fomething hereafter.

By this Difcourfe it is Evident againft Mr. *Hobbs*, and others of the Sadducean Opinion, that Spirits in their own Nature
are

are Real and *Subsistent Beings,* and not meerly *Powers,* or *Operations* and *Actions*; tho' at the same time it must be acknowledged, that in the Language of the *Scripture,* such *Active* and *Directive* Qualities as are *Intelligible* only, and do not come directly within the Cognizance of the sense are called *Spirits*; thus we read of a Spirit of *Government* and of *Prophecy,* that was first upon *Moses,* and afterward imparted to the 70 Elders, *Numb.* 11. of a Spirit of *Wisdom, Deut.* 34. 9. of the Spirit of *Understanding*; the Spirit of *Counsel* and *Might*; the Spirit of *Knowledge,* and of the *Fear* of the Lord, *Isa.* 11. 2. Ay, that vexatious Distemper that afflicted *Saul,* and that seems to have been nothing else but melancholly, is called an Evil Spirit from the Lord, 1 *Sam.* 16. 14. and in *Luke* 13. 11, 12. we read of a Spirit of *Infirmity.*

But tho' Spirit in the Holy Scriptures is often taken in the instanced sense; and that the *Name* of *Angel* is a Name of *Office,* rather than of *Nature*; yet it is certain, that Angels are represented in those Sacred Writings as *Real* subsisting Beings, all as real and subsisting as men themselves are, if the ascribing to *them* the like Affections, Offices, and Personal Operations, that

Men

Men have, and do execute and exert, can prove them so.

SECT. II.

That there are Spirits, proved by General Tradition. Mr. Hobb's *Answer to this Argument shewed to be but an Evasion, from the Evangelists* Matthew, *and* Mark, *&c.*

AND this reminds me of the *Second* Point I have proposed to Discourse on, in relation to Spirits, and that is, their *Existence* or Being; wherein I shall endeavour to make it manifest, that really there are such Subsistent intellectual Beings, as are incorporated, but invisible, which commonly we call *Spirits*; so that the Names of Spirits, both of the Good ones, as *Raphael, Gabriel, &c.* And of the Evil ones, as *Belzebub, &c.* are Names of *Substances* or Persons, and not of Qualities only; ay, are *proper*, and not (as Mr. *Hobbs* tells us, the name of *Sathan* and *Devil* is) only *Appellative* Names.

The first Argument that I will use to Evidence that there are Spirits, shall be taken from the *General Tradition* of the World; it being received among all *Nations*, as well the Civilized, as the Barbarous,

rous, and among all *Philosophers* except the *Epicureans*, the Ancient and the Modern, and *some* Peripateticks; and to me it is very unintelligible, how such a Sentiment shou'd obtain so generally, if it had not some foundation of Truth; for *who* should spread the Opinion to such an extent? and *what* should make it to take?

Mr. *Hobbs* himself acknowledges it a truth, that the belief of Spirits was very general all the World over; only he has a way (which is peculiar to him) of avoiding the Cogency and Force of the Argument, and therefore I will here consider what he says.

It is true, says he, 'that the *Heathens*, 'and all the Nations of the World have 'acknowledged that there be Spirits, which 'for the most part they hold to be incorporeal, whereby it may be thought that 'a man by natural Reason may arrive 'without the Scriptures to the knowledge 'of this, that Spirits are, but the erroneous Collection thereof by the Heathens, 'may proceed as I have said before, from 'the ignorance of the Cause of Ghosts and 'Fantoms, and such other Apparitions. 'And from thence had the *Grecians* their 'number of Gods, their number of Demons good, or bad, and for every Man 'his Genius, which is not the acknowledging

'ing of this truth, that Spirits are, but a
'falſe Opinion concerning the force of Ima-
'gination.

Thus Mr. *Hobbs*, in his Treatiſe of Human Nature, *Ch.* 11. *S.* 6. wherein he plainly Affirms, that Spirits and Ghoſts are meer Fantomes, or Effects of the Imagination: a conceit, in which he ſeems to have the Concurrence of *Seneca*, for this Philoſopher Epiſt. 24. tells us as Mr. *Hobbs* doe's, *Nemo tam Puer eſt ut Cerberum timeat, & Tenebras, & LARVARUM habitum nudis oſſibus Cohærentium.*

This *Notion* of Spirits, that Mr. *Hobbs* Inſinuates, Reminds me of *Another*, that a Perſon whom I knew, and who was Reputed not of the Wiſeſt, had of them; for being Asked what he thought a *Spirit* was, He Anſwered, that it was the *Shadow of Conſcience*; and further Demanded, concerning a *Good Angel*, what that was; He Replied, a Good is the Shadow of a *Good* Conſcience, and a *Devil* the Shadow of a *Bad* one, And Methinks he comes near to Mr. *Hobbs*. But without jeſting.

I Find, that *Apparitions* of Spirits are ſtiled *Fantoms* [φαντάσματα] by two Evangeliſts, *Matthew* and *Mark*. For when the Diſciples of our Lord ſaw him walking upon the Sea, and believed him to be a Spirit, the Former of thoſe Evangeliſts tells us us that they said ὅτι φάντασμα ἐστί, it is a Phantasm, or, as our Translators Render it, a *Sprite*, *Matt*. 14. 26. And the Latter has the same Expression, when speaking of the same Miracle, he says, they supposed him to be a *Phantasm*, ἔδοξαν φάντασμα εἶναι; or as in our English Version, they *supposed it had been a* Sprite. *Mark*. 6. 49. Whence it Evidently follows, against Mr. *Hobbs*, that Men that were not Ignorant of the power of *Fancy*, and of the Interest it had in the Apparitions of Spirits, yet believed their *Real* Existence. For the Disciples that believed our Lord to be a Spirit, *Appearing*, and therefore said he was a *Phantasm* (which it seems was the usual Expression at that time for such Apparitions,) did withal believe that a Spirit was a *Reality*, and of great Power. For upon the supposed Apparition, They are said, by *one* of the Evangelists, to be much *Disturbed*, ἐταράχθησαν says *Matthew*, Chap. 14. 26. They were *troubled* and cryed out *for Fear*; and the *other* says no less, for he says, *They cried out*, (*for They all saw him and were* Troubled,) *Mark*. 6. 49, 50. I would Demand of Mr. *Hobbs*, were he Alive, what can be Conceived to occasion so much Consternation, so much Affrightment, in the Disciples, at the Apparition of a Spirit,

if

if they did not take a Spirit to be something Real, tho' they called the Appearing of it a Phantome. Certainly, when they were so much Affrighted at it, They must be Apprehensive that it was a Thing of Great Power, that was come to hurt Them; for else, had They believed it to be a meer Effect of Their own Imagination, they would have been as *Unconcerned*, as Mr. *Hobbs* himself would be, at such an Appearance.

I Conclude then, that as Mr. *Hobbs* was not the First that called Spirits *Phantasmata*, or Fantomes, but that they were called so of Old, (and indeed the word *Spectrum* in the Latin, and this of *Apparition* in the English Tongue, does answer very Properly to the word *Phantasma* in the Greek, a word too Adopted by the *Romans*, in the same sense;) so this Denomination was Given to them, not with Design to signify their *Nature* and Essence, (as Mr. *Hobbs* would have it,) but to set out the usual *way* of Their Appearing, of which more hereafter. This is Evident from the Younger *Pliny*, who in one of his Epistles, having put the Question, whether Apparitions or *Phantasmata* (for this is the word he uses) were Real and subsistent Things, he Affirms they are, and Instances in several Remarkable Stories

ries (as I shall shew hereafter) to Prove it.

So that this First Argument for the Real Existence of Spirits, taken from the General belief that all the World has of it (as Mr. *Hobbs* himself Acknowledges,) doe's hold Good and Conclusive, Notwithstanding all that this Philosopher has suggested against it. And indeed what he Proposes, is said so *Timorously* by him, [for he say's, *the Erroneous Collection thereof may* [but may] *Proceed* &c.] and that so *Precariously*, (being only an Assertion, without any Proof), that I need not have Given my self the trouble of saying so much in Answer to it, but that in Things of this Nature, some have so very strong a Byass, both of *Credulity* on one hand, and *Incredulity* on the other, that if any Room were left for Cavil, they would be sure to make it.

SUB. I.

Another Argument to Prove Spirits. Of the Conversion of an Indian *Raja. A Remarkable Story of Witchcraft, out of* Mr. Gage's *Survey.*

AND Thus much for the First Argument, I now proceed to the second. And the second Argument that I will use to Evidence that there are Spirits, shall be taken from *Operations* we are certain of, which cannot be Accounted for but by supposing such Agents.

I have Read in *Purchas*, that a certain *Indian*, a Great *Raja*, and Greater *Atheist*, was brought to a Confession, as well as Conviction of his Folly, by a strange Providence. The Relation in that Author, goes in these Terms. " A Great *Raja* a
" Gentile, a Notorious *Atheist*, and Con-
" temner of all Deity, Glorying to pro-
" fess he knew no other *God* than the
" *King*, nor believing nor fearing none:
" sitting Dallying with his Women, one
" of them plucked a *Hair* from his Breast,
" which being fast Rooted, Plucked off a
" little of the Skin, that Blood Appear-
" ed; this small Skar Festred and Gan-
" grened Incurably, so that in few days
" he

" he Despaired of Life, and being Ac-
" companied with all his Friends and
" Divers Courtiers he brake out into these
" Excellent words: Which of you would
" not have Thought that I being a Man of
" War should have died by the Stroak of
" a Sword, Spear, or Bow? But now
" I am enforced to confess the Power of
" that *Great God*, whom I have so long
" Despised, that he needs no other *Lance*
" than a little Hair to kill so *Blasphemous*
" a wretch and Contemner of his Majesty,
" as I have been. *Part.* 1. *l.* 4. *f.* 600.
Thus God, is known in the World, by the *Judgments* which he Executes

And as God is known by his Judgments, so may other Spirits, by some *Events* that happen in the World, when they are so Extraordinary, and out of common course, that they cannot be Ascribed but to such Causes. I have here a very Large Field, but my Business being not to handle this Subject as a Common Place, but only to Touch it by way of Argument, I shall content my self with the General Mention of *Prodigies*, that all History, Ancient and Modern, abounds withal; and the strange Performances of *Witches* and Wizards; of which Last I will give an *Instance* or two, that carry great Credibility, and yet are Absolutely
Unaccount-

Unaccountable, if we do not Admit of Spirits, and in Truth not very Easy to be Conceived if we do. But the Matter of *Fact*, being Related by an Author not in every Bodies hand, I will lay it out at large in all its Circumstances, as I Find them set down by him, that so Ingenious Men, who have the Curiosity to Inquire into Things of this Nature, may have the surer Grounds to go upon, in making their Judgment.

In *Pinola* (say's Mr. *Gage* in his new Survey of the *West-Indies*, C. 20.) there were some who were much given to Witchcraft, and by the Power of the Devil did Act strange things; amongst the Rest there was one Old Woman Named *Martha de Carillo*, who had been by some of the Town formerly Accused for Bewitching many; but the *Spanish* Justices quitted her, finding no sure Evidence against her; with this she grew worse and worse, and did much Harm; when I was there, two or three died, *withering away*, Declaring at their Death that this *Carillo* had Killed them, and that they *saw her* often about their Beds, threatning them with a Frowning and Angry Look. The *Indians* for fear of her durst not complain against her, nor meddle with her; whereupon I sent word unto *Don Juan de Guzman* the Lord of that Town, that if he took not order with her, she would destroy his Town. He Hearing of it, got for me a Commission from the Bishop and another Officer of the Inquisition to make Diligent and Private Inquiry after her Life and Actions, which I did, and found among the *Indians* many and Grievous Complaints against her, most of the Town Affirming that certainly she was a Notorious Witch, and that before her former Accusation she was wont withersoever she went about the Town to go with a *Duck* Following her, which when she came to the Church would stay at the door till she came out again, and then would Return home with her, which Duck they Imagined was her Beloved Devil and Familiar Spirit, for that they had often set Dogs at her and they would not meddle with her, but rather run away from her. This Duck never Appeared more with her, *since* she was formerly Accused before the Justice, which was thought to be her policy, that she might be no more suspected thereby. This Old Woman was a Widow, and of the *Poorest* of the Town in outward shew, and yet she had always store of *Money*, which none could tell which way she might come by it. Whilst I was thus Taking Privy Information against

against her (it being the Time of *Lent*, when all the Town came to Confeſſion) ſhe among the Reſt came to the Church to *Confeſs* her ſins, and brought me the beſt Preſent and Offering of all the Town; for whereas a Riall is Common, ſhe brought me four, and beſides, a *Turkey, Eggs, Fiſh*, and a little Bottle of *Honey*. She thought thereby to get with me a better Opinion than I had of her from the whole Town. I Accepted of her Great Offering, and heard her Confeſſion, which was of nothing but Trifles, which could ſcarce be Judged ſinful Actions. I Examined her very cloſe of what was the Common Judgment of all the *Indians*, and eſpecially of thoſe who dying, had declared to my ſelf *at their Death* that She had Bewitched them, and before their Sickneſs had *Threatned* them, and in their Sickneſs *Appeared* Threatning them with Death about their beds, none but they themſelves ſeeing her; to which ſhe Replyed Weeping that ſhe was Wronged. I Asked her, *how* ſhe being a Poor Widow without any Sons to help her, without any means of Livelyhood, had ſo much Money, as to give me more than the Richeſt of the Town; *how* She came by that Fiſh, Turkey, and Honey, having none of this of her own about her Houſe? to which ſhe *Replied*, that

that God Loved her and gave her all thefe Things, and that with her Money fhe Bought the reft. I *Asked* her *of whom?* She *Anfwered* that out of the Town fhe had them. I Perfuaded her to much Repentance, and to forfake the Devil and all Fellowfhip with him; but her Words and Anfwers were of a Saintly and Holy Woman; and fhe earneftly defired me to give her the *Communion* with the Reft that were to Receive the next day. Which I told her I durft not do, ufing Chrift's Words, Give not the Childrens bread unto dogs, nor caft your Pearls unto Swine; and it would be a great Scandal to give the Communion unto her, who was fufpected generally, and had been Accufed for a *Witch*. This fhe took very ill, telling me that fhe had many Years *Received* the Communion, and now in her Old Age it Grieved her to be Deprived of it, her tears were many, yet I could not be moved with them, but Refolutely denied her the Communion, and fo Difmiffed her. At Noon when I had done my work in the Church, I bad my Servants go to gather up the Offerings, and gave order to have the *Fifh* Dreffed for my Dinner which fhe had brought, but no fooner was it carried into the Kitchen, when the Cook looking on it found it *full of Maggots*, and ftinking; fo that

that I was forced to hurl it away; with that I began to fupect my Old Witch, and went to look on her *Honey*, and Pouring it out into a Dish, I found it full of *Worms*; her *Eggs* I could not know from others, there being near a Hundred Offered that day, but after as I ufed them, we found fome *Rotten*, fome with *dead Chickens* in them; the next Morning the *Turkey* was found dead; As for her four *Rials*, I could not Perceive whether fhe had Bewitched them out of my Pocket, for that I had put them with many other, which that day had been given Given me, yet as far as I could I called to Memory *who* and *what* had been Given me, and in my Judgment and Reckoning I verily thought that I miffed *four* Rials; At Night when my Servants the *Indians* were gone to Bed, I fat up late in my Chamber betaking my felf to my Books and Study, for I was the next Morning to make an Exhortation to thofe that Received the Communion. After I had Studied a while, it being between Ten and Eleven of the Clock; on a fudden the *Chief door* in the Hall (where in a Lower Room was my Chamber, and the Servants, and *three other* doors) flew *open*, and I heard one *come in*, and for a while *walk about*; then was *Another* door opened which went into a Little Room,

where

where my Saddles were Laid; with this I thought it might be the Black-More *Miguel Dalva*, who would often come late to my House to Lodge there, Especially since my fear of *Montenegro*, and I Conjectured that he was Laying up his Saddle, I called unto him by his Name two or three times, from within my Chamber, but no Answer was made, but suddenly *Another door* that went out to a Garden flew also open, wherewith I began within to *fear*, my joynts Trembled, my Hair stood up, I would have called out to the Servants, and my Voice was as it were stopped with the sudden Affrightment; I began to think of the Witch, and put my trust in God against her. and Encouraged my self and Voice, calling out to the Servants, and knocking with a Cane at my door within that they might hear me, for I durst not open it and go out; with the Noise that I made the Servants Awaked, and came out to my Chamber door; then I opened it, and asked them if they had not heard some Body in the Hall, and all the doors opened, they said they were Asleep, and heard nothing, only one *Boy* said he *heard all*, and Related unto me the *same* that I had heard; I took my Candle then in my hand and went out with them into the Hall to view the *doors*, and I found them all

all *shut,* as the Servants said they had left them. Then I Perceived that the *Witch* would have Affrighted me, but had no power to do me any harm; I made two of the Servants lie in my Chamber, and went to bed; in the morning early I sent for my *Fiscal* the Clerk of the Church, and told him what had happen'd that Night, he smiled upon me, and told me it was the Widdow *Carillo,* who had often played such Tricks in the Town with those that had offended her, and therefore he had the night before come unto me from her, desiring me to give her the Communion, left she should do me some hurt, which I denied unto him, as I had done to her self; the Clerk bad me be of good cheer, for he knew she had no power over me to do me any hurt. After the Communion that day, some of the Chief *Indians* came unto me, and told me that Old *Carillo* had *Boasted* that she would play me *some trick* or other, because I would not give her the Communion. But I, to rid the Town of such a Limb of Satan, sent her to *Guatemala,* with all the Evidences and Witnesses which I had found against her, unto the President and Bishop, who commanded her to be put in Prison, where she died within two months.

Many more *Indians* there were in that Town, who were said in my time to do very *strange* things. One called *John Gonzalez*, was reported to *Change* himself into the shape of a Lion, and in that shape was one day shot in the nose by a poor harmless *Spaniard*, who chiefly got his living by going about the Woods and Mountains, and shooting at Wild Deer, and other Beasts to make Mony of them. He espied one day a *Lion*, and having no other aim at him but his Snout behind a Tree, he shot at him, the *Lion* ran away; the same day this *Gonzalez* was taken sick; I was sent for to hear his Confession, I saw his face and nose all bruised, and asked *how it came?* he told me then that he had fallen from a Tree, and almost killed himself, yet afterwards he accused the poor *Spaniard* for shooting at him; the business was examined by a *Spanish* Justice, my Evidence was taken for what *Gonzalez* told me of his fall from a Tree; the *Spaniard* was put to his Oath, who swore that he shot at a Lion in a Thick Wood, where an *Indian* could scarce be thought to have any business; the Tree was found out in the Wood, whereat the shot had been made, and was still marked with the shot and Bullet; which *Gonzalez* confessed was to be the place; and was Examined how

he

he neither fell nor was seen by the *Spaniard*, when he came to seek for the Lion, thinking he had killed him; to which he answered, that he ran away left the *Spaniard* should kill him indeed. But his Answers seemed frivolous, the *Spaniards* integrity being known, and the great suspicion that was in the Town, of *Gonzalez* his dealing with the Devil, cleared the *Spaniard* from what was laid against him.

But this was nothing to what after happened to one *John Gomez*, the chiefest Indian of that Town of near fourscore years of Age, the Head and Ruler of the Principalleft Tribe among the *Indians*, whose Advice and Counsel was taken and preferred before all the rest; who seemed to be a very *Godly* Indian, and very seldom missed Morning and Evening Prayers in the Church, and had bestowed great Riches there. This *Indian* very suddenly was taken sick (I being then in my other Town of *Mixco*) the *Mayordomos* or Stewards of the Sodality of the Virgin, fearing that he might die without Confession, and they be chid for their negligence, at Midnight called me up at *Mixco*, desiring me to go presently and help *John Gomez* to die, whom also they said desired much to see me, and to receive some comfort from me.

me. I judging it a work of Charity, although the time of the night were unseasonable, and the great Rain at the present might have stopped my Charity, yet I would not be hindred by either of them, and so set forth to ride nine Miles both in the Dark, and Wet. When I came to *Pinola*, being thorow wet to the skin, I went immediately to the House of Old Sick *Gomez*, who lay with his face all muffled up, thanked me for my pains and care I had for his Soul, he desired to confess, and by his Confession and Weeping Evidenced nothing but a Godly Life, and a willing desire to die, and to be with Christ, I comforted him, and prepared him for Death, and before I departed, asked him how he felt himself; he answered that his Sickness was nothing but Old Age, and Weakness; with this I went to my House, changed my self, and lay down a while to rest, when suddenly I was called up again to give *Gomez* the Extream Unction, which the *Indians* (as they have been ignorantly taught) will not omit to receive before they die. As I Anointed him in his Nose, his Lips, his Eyes, his Hands and his Feet, I perceived that he was swelled, and black and blew, but made nothing of it, judging it to proceed from the sickness of his Body; I went home

home again, being now break of the day, when after I had taken a small nap, some *Indians* came to my door to buy Candles to offer up for *John Gomez* his Soul, whom they told me was departed, and was that day to be Buried very solemnly at Mass. I arose with drousie Eyes after so unquiet a nights rest; and walked to the Church, where I saw the Grave was preparing. I met with two or three *Spaniards* who lived near the Town, and were come to Mass that Morning, who went in with me to my Chamber, and with them I fell into Discourse about *John Gomez*, telling them what comfort I had received at his Death, whom I judged to have lived very Holy, and doubted not of his Salvation, and that the Town would much want him, for that he was their Chief Guide, and Leader, Ruling them with good Advice and Counsel. At this time the *Spaniards* smiled one at another, and told me I was much deceived by all the *Indians*, but especially by the deceased *Gomez*, if I judged him to have been a Saint, and Holy Man. I told them, that they, as Enemies to the *Indians*, judged still uncharitably of them; but that I who knew very well their Consciences, could judge better of them than they. One then Replyed, that it seemed I little knew the truth of *John Gomez*

Gomez his death by the Confeſſion which he made unto me, and that I ſeemed to be ignorant of the ſtir which was made in the Town concerning his Death. This ſeemed ſo ſtrange unto me, that I deſired them to inform me of the Truth. Then they told me that the report went, that *John Gomez* was the Chief *Wizard* of all the *Wizards* and *Witches* in the Town, and that commonly he was wont to be changed into the ſhape of a *Lion*, and ſo to walk about the Mountains. That he was ever a deadly Enemy to one *Sebaſtian Lopez* an Ancient *Indian*, and head of another Tribe; and that both of them two days before had met in the Mountain. *Gomez* in the ſhape of a *Lion*, and *Lopez* in the ſhape of a *Tyger*; and that they fought moſt cruelly, till *Gomez* (who was the older and weaker) was tired, much bit and bruiſed, and died of it. And farther, that I might be aſſured of this truth, they told me that *Lopez* was in Priſon for it, and the two Tribes ſtriving about it, and that the Tribe and Kindred of *Gomez* demanded from *Lopez* and his Tribe and Kindred ſatisfaction, and a great Sum of Money, or elſe did threaten to make the Caſe known unto the Spaniſh Power and Authority, which yet they were unwilling to do, if they could agree and ſmother it up among them-

themselves, that they might not bring an aspersion upon their whole Town. This seemed very strange unto me, and I could not resolve what to believe, and thought I would never more believe an *Indian*, if I found *John Gomez* to have so much Dissembled and Deceived me. I took my leave of the *Spaniards*, and went my self to the Prison, where I found *Lopez* with Fetters. I called one of the Officers of the Town, who was *Alguazil Major*, and my great Friend, unto my House, and privately examined him why *Lopez* was kept so close Prisoner? he was loath to tell me, fearing the rest of the *Indians*, and hoping the business would be taken up and agreed by the two Tribes, and not noised about the Country, which at that instant the two Alcades and Regidores, Majors, and Jurates, with the Chief of both Tribes were sitting about in the Town-House all that Morning. But I seeing the Officer so timorous, was more desirous to know something, and pressed more upon him for the Truth, giving him an inkling of what I had heard from the *Spaniards* before. To which he answered, that if they could agree amongst themselves, they feared no ill report from the *Spaniards* against their Town; I told him I must know what they were agreeing upon amongst them-

themselves so closely in the Town-House. He told me, if I would promise to say nothing of him (for he feared the whole Town if they should know he had revealed any thing unto me) he would tell me the Truth. With this I comforted him, and gave him a Cup of Wine, and encouraged him, warranting him that no harm should come unto him for what he told me. Then he related the business unto me as the *Spaniards* had done, and told me that he thought the Tribes amongst themselves would not agree; for that some of *Gomez* his Friends hated *Lopez*, and all such as were so Familiar with the Devil, and cared not if *Gomez* his dissembling Life were laid open to the World; but others he said, who were as bad as *Lopez*, and *Gomez*, would have kept it close, left they, and all the Witches and Wizards in the Town should be discovered. This struck me to the very heart, to think that I should live amongst such People, whom I saw were spending all they could get by their Work and Labour upon the Church, Saints, and in Offerings, and yet were so privy to the Counsels of Satan; it grieved me that the word I preached unto them did no more good; and I resolved from that time forward to spend most of my indeavours against Satans subtilty, and
to

to shew them more than I had done, the great danger of their Souls who had made any Compact with the Devil, that I might make them abandon and abjure his Works, and close with Christ by Faith. *I* dismissed the *Indian*, and went to the Church to see if the People were come to Mass; I found there no body but only two who were making *Gomez* his Grave. I went back to my Chamber, troubled much within my self, whether I should allow him a Christian Burial, who had lived and died so wickedly, as I had been informed. Yet I thought I was not bound to believe one *Indian* against him, nor the *Spaniards*, whom I supposed spoke but by hear-say. Whilst I was thus musing, there came unto me at least twenty of the Chiefest of the Town, with the two Majors, Jurates, and all the Officers of Justice, who desired me to forbear that day the Burying of *John Gomez*, for that they had resolved to call a Crown Officer to view his Corps, and examine his death, lest they should all be troubled for him, and he be again unburied. I made as if I knew nothing, but inquired of them the reason; then they related all unto me, and told me how there were Witnesses in the Town, who *saw a Lyon and a Tyger Fighting*, and presently lost the sight of the Beasts, and *saw John Gomez, and Sebastian Lopez*, much about the same time parting one from another, and that immediately *John Gomez* came home bruised to his Bed, from whence he never rose more, and that he declared upon his Death-Bed unto some of his Friends that *Sebastian Lopez* had killed him; whereupon they had him in safe Custody. Farther they told me, that though they had never known so much wickedness of these two Chief Heads of their Town whom they had much respected and followed; yet now upon this occasion, from the one Tribe and the other they were certainly informed that both of them did constantly deal with the Devil, which would be a great aspersion upon their Town, but they for their parts abjured all such wicked ways, and prayed me not to conceive the worse of all for a few, whom they were resolved to persecute, and not suffer to live amongst them. I told them I much liked their good zeal, and incouraged them as good Christians to endeavour the rooting out of Satan from their Town, and they did very well in giving notice to *Guatemala*, to the *Spanish* Power of this Accident; and that if they had concealed it, they might all have been punished as guilty of *Gomez* his death, and Agents with Satan, and his Instruments.

I assured them I had no ill conceit of them, but rather judged well of them for what they agreed to do. The Crown Officer was sent for, who came that night and searched *Gomez* his Body; I was present with him, and found it all *bruised*, scratched, and in many places *Bitten* and sore wounded. Many Evidences and suspicions were brought in against *Lopez* by the *Indians* of the Town, especially by *Gomez*, his Friends, whereupon he was carryed away to *Guatemala*, and there again was Tryed by the same Witnesses, and not much Denying the Fact himself, was there *Hanged*. And *Gomez*, though his Grave was opened in the Church, he was not Buried in it, but in another made Ready for him in a Ditch. So far in *Gage*.

There are multitudes of *Instances* in many Authors, of a Nature all as strange, and as surprizing, as the former; and *tho'* perhaps *most* of the Relations handed about with great Confidence, do, upon impartial Examination, prove either *Impostures* of Malicious, or *Mistakes* of Ignorant and Superstitious Persons; yet some come so well Attested, that it were to bid defiance to all Human Testimony to refuse them belief. Among Forreign Writers I will mention only the Learned & Judicious *Bodin* in his *Dæmonomania*, and the Curious *Gasper Schottus* in his *Physica Curiosa*, Part 1. C. 16. § 3. and C. 17. § 2. Among our own, the Eloquent Mr. *Glanvil*, in his *Sadducismus Triumphatus*; and Mr. *Baxter* (as Sagacious and Inquisitive a person as any) his *Historical Discourse* of Apparitions and Witches, who all abound with very Prodigious, but Credible Relations. To all which I might add the Confessions I have in Manuscript, (all Original Papers, and well vouched,) of a great number of Witches, (some of which were Executed) that were taken by a *Justice* of Peace in *Cornwall* above thirty Years agoe: In which there are so many Rare and Curious Passages, that I find my self under great Temptation of Promising to Annex them to the Second Part of this Discourse, when I shall have Occasion to say more upon the present Subject, under the Head of Supernatural Power. And Thus much for the *Second* Argument, which leads me to the *Third*.

SUB. I.

SUBS. II.

The Third Argument from Supernatural Advertisements. An Instance out of Simocatto. *Another, of a strange Omen out of Sir* W. Rawleigh. *Of the Corps-Candles in* Wales, *&c.*

THE Third Argument to prove the Real Being of Spirits, shall be taken from the strange *Advertisements* of Events, and as strange *Premonitions*, that are sometimes Given, which cannot be Resolved but upon that *Hypothesis*. I will but mention the *Oracles* of Old; the many Admonishing and Predictive *Dreams*, that some Persons, in all Ages, have been Favoured with, (of which there is a Large Collection by *Strozzo Cicogna* in his *Magia Omnifariâ*, Part 1. l. 2. C. 4. as also in *Cicero*, in his First Book of Divination;) and in fine, the Prodigious *Omens* that do often occur.

Nor will I insist on what I find in Mr. *Stow* and other Historians, that *William*, Surnamed the Conquerour, though he died at *Roan* in *Normandy*, sooner than was Expected, yet his Death was known at *Rome* the same day he Died. But I lay more stress upon an *Advertisement* I find in

Theophylact

Theophylact Simocatta, concerning the Murther of the Emperour *Mauritius*, because the Relation of it being Particular and Circumstantial, carries Greater Evidence than the Former, and will endure the Test. There happened, says the *Historian*, on the very day in which *Mauritius* [the Emepror] was Murdred, a thing at *Alexandria* worthy to be Recorded. A certain Writing-Master or Scrivener (for so I do Adventure to interpret the word *Calligraphus*) being (that day) at a Merchants House at a kind of Gossips Feast, where he was obliged to stay till the Fourth Watch of the Night; as he was going homeward, being come to the *Tychaum*, a noted part of the City, (about midnight) he saw some of the chiefest *Statues* that stood there removing from off their Bases, and at the same time heard a *Voice* that seemed to come from the same Statues, which called on him aloud, by Name, and withal, very shrilly, but briefly, Related the Accident that that day had befaln *Mauritius*. In the morning the Writing-Master goes to the Palace to Discover what had happened to him, which coming to the Ear of *Peter* the Prefect of *Ægypt* then residing there (who was nearly Related to *Simocatta*) he diligently inquires concerning the whole Affair, and

and after he had fully informed himself thereof, injoyns the Relater to Secrecy, and then setting down, in his Note Book, the whole Relation, he waits the Event. Of this not long after, he was assured by an Express, which on the Ninth day brought him News of the Emperours *Death*, and of the Time of it; and then he Declared Publickly, how that this Accident had been *Foretold* by the Statues, or rather by the Demons, in the manner above Related, and Vouched the Writing-Master as the Author. This is the sum of the Story, as *Simocatta* has Related it, (*Hist. Mauritian. l.* 8. *Ch.* 13.) A Story that is not told at Random, or by an Obscure Person, or by a Person Remote from the Scene, or from the time it was Acted on; but a Story told by a Grave and Understanding Historian, who lived at the same time; was well acquainted with the Persons concerned; and who made a Figure in the Government; so that he had all the Advantages that could be desired to render him certain of the truth of it. *Lucilius* in *Cicero L.* 2. *de Nat. Deor.* tells us a story of the like Nature, *viz.* That the Elder *P. Vatienus* coming by night to *Rome*, was Advertized by the *Tyndarida* in the shape of two young men, on White Horses, that that day *Perses* was overcome

come by the Roman Army, and taken Prisoner; This he Reports to the Senate, by whom he was committed to Prison for spreading False News; but afterwards, when it Appeared by the Consuls Letters, that the Advertisement was true, he was both Released and Rewarded.

And as for *Omens*, than which nothing is more Ridiculous to the *Epicureans*, and all those that deny the Reality of Spirits, (so says *Cicero* de Nat. Deor. l. 2. *Nihil tam Ierridet* Epicurus *quam Prædictionem rerum futurarum*;) I will Instance in one that leaves no Room for any Evasion, since I take it from a Person who was very Confident of the Truth of it, and yet was a Person as little subject to Superstition, or to Fancy, as any Epicurean whatever. Sir *Walter Rawleigh* (for it is he I mean) in his History of the World (*B.* 4. *C.* 2. *S.* 7.) says,
'The strangest thing that I have Read of
' in this kind [*speaking of Omens*] being
' *certainly* true, was, that the Night be-
' fore the Battle at *Novara*, All, [*not one,*
' *or some, which might be Chance, but All,*]
' the Doggs which Followed the *French*
' Army Ran from them to the *Switzers*,
' Leaping and Fawning upon them, as if
' they had been Bred and Fed by them
' all their Lives. And in the Morning
' Following, *Trivulzi* and *Tremovilli* Gene-
' rals

'ralls for *Lewis* the 12th were by these
'Imperial *Switzers* utterly Broken and
'put to Ruine.

But to Proceed, What will an *Epicurean*, or meer *Somatist*, say to the *Corps-Candles*, or Dead Mens Lights in *Wales*? if all be true that is Reported of them in Mr. *B*'s. Historical Discourse, *Ch. 6.* And Methinks his Vouchers are Good. I will Relate the Account they give in their own Terms; The First is one Mr. *Lewis*, who in his First Letter to Mr. *B.* (*October* 20. 1656.) speaking of the Appearance of those Lights which are called *Dead-Mens Candles*, before Mortality, He says, 'This is so or-
'dinary in most of our Counties [of
'*Wales*] that I never scarce heard of any
'sort young or old, but this is seen be-
'fore Death, and often observed to part
'from the very Bodies of the Persons, all
'along the way to the Place of Burial, and
'Infallibly Death will Ensue. In his *Third*
'Letter Dated *Febr.* 14. 1656. He says,
'as for the *Candles*, all the Parts I know
'of *Wales*, as our Neighbouring Counties
'(as I hear) have Experience of them, I
'scarce know any Gentleman, or Minister
'of any standing, but hath seen them;
'and a Neighbour of mine, will shortly
'be at *Worcester* Abiding (who hath seen
'them often, and I will Direct some to
'Acquaint

'Acquaint you, and upon Oath, if need
'be,) a very Credible Aged Person; for
'my Part, I never saw the Candles;
'but those of my House have, and on a
'Time some two years Past, it was told
'me by them, that Two Candles were
'seen, one Little, and a Great one, Pas-
'sing the Church way, under my House,
'my Wife was then great with Child, and
'near her time, and she Feared of it, and
'it Begat some fear in us about her, but
'just about a Week after, her self first
'came to me (as something joyed that the
'Fear might be over) and said (as true it
'was) an Old Man, and a Child of the
'Neighbourhood Passed that same way to
'be Buried. This she and I can Depose.

Thus that Gentleman; who at that time (as Mr. B. stiles him) was a Learned Justice of Peace, and seems by his Letters to have been a very Cautious Circumspect Person, and a Person of Great Veracity, and therefore a Person who cannot be Imagined to go about to Deceive, or that could be Deceived himself in a matter Represented to him (as this was) as of General observation. For it was Easie for him to know if the thing were of so General Observation or Note, (since it was but to Ask People,) and if it was, it could not be False, as having the Testimony of common

mon Knowledge and Experience to Avow it; and if it was not, it would be Temerity in him to believe it true; since it wanted even that Evidence that was Pretended to ground it; but it seems the Gentleman Inquired, and found the thing Confirmed (as he says) by General Experience, and I believe him too Honest to say it, if it had not been so. Besides, what he mentions in Relation to his Wife and Family, if well Considered, Adds no little strength to the whole Story. And in Fine, he brings one Mr. *Davis* for his Voucher.

This Mr. *Davis* in a Letter that he wrote to Mr. *B.* at the Request of Mr. *Lewis*, is more particular and Full than that Gentleman, in Reference to those Lights, and therefore (the Matter being Rare and Curious, and well Deserving to be made a subject of Inquiry by the Noblest Wits) I will Transcribe it at Large. ' I am to
' give you, says he, the Best Satisfaction I
' can touching these *Fiery Apparitions*,
' which do as it were mark out the way
' for Corpses to their Κοιμητήρια, and that
' sometimes before the *parties* themselves fall
' Sick, and sometimes in their Sickness. Of
' These I could never hear in *England*,
' they are Common in these Three Coun-
' ties, *Cardigan, Caermarthen*, and *Pembrooke*,
' and

'and as I hear, in some other Parts of *Wales*.

'These φαντάσμαλα in our Language
'we call *Cankwyllau Cyrth* (*i.e.*) Corps-
'Candles; and *Candles* we call them, not
'that we do see any thing else besides
'the Light, but because that Light doth
'as much Resemble a Material Can-
'dle Light, as Eggs do Eggs, saving that
'in their journey, these Candles be
'*modò Apparentes*, modò *Disparentes*, Es-
'pecially, when one comes near them;
'and if one come on the way against them,
'unto him they vanish; but presently ap-
'pear behind him, and hold on their
'Course. If it be a *little* Candle, Pale or
'Blewish, then follows the Corps either
'of an *Abortive*, or some *Infant*, if a *Big*
'one, then the Corps of some one *come to*
'*Age*; if there be seen *two*, or three, or
'more, some Big, some Small together,
'then so many, and such Corps together;
'if two Candles come from Divers Places,
'and be seen to meet, the Corpses will
'the like, if any of these Candles be
'seen to turn sometimes a little out
'of the way, or Path that Leadeth unto
'the Church, the following Corps will be
'found to turn in that very Place, for the
'Avoiding of some Dirty Lane, or Plash, *&c.*
'Now let us fall to Evidence, being about
'the Age of Fifteen, Dwelling at *Lanylar*,
'late

' late at Night, some Neighbours saw one
' of these Candles Hovering up and down
' along the River Bank until they were
' weary in Beholding, at last they left it
' so, and went to Bed, a few Weeks after
' came a Proper Damsel from *Montgomery*
' *Shire*, to see her Friends, who Dwelt
' on the other side of that River *Istwyth*,
' and thought to Ford the River at that
' very Place where the Light was seen;
' but being Dissuaded by some Lookers on,
' (some its most like of those that saw the
' Light) to Adventure on the Water, which
' was High by Reason of a Flood; she walked
' up and down along the River Bank, even
' where, and even as the foresaid Candle
' did, waiting for the Falling of the Water,
' which at last she took, but too soon for
' her, for she was Drown'd therein

' Of Late, my Sexton's Wife, an Aged
' Understanding Woman, saw from her
' Bed, a little Blewish Candle upon her
' Tables end, within two or three days
' after, comes a Fellow in, Enquiring for
' her Husband, and taking something
' from under his Cloak, claps it down
' directly upon the Tables end, where she
' had seen the Candle, and what was it
' but a Dead born Child: Another time
' the same Woman, saw such Another
' Candle upon the other end of the self
' same

' same Table, within few days after, a
' Weak Child, by my felf newly Chrift-
' ned, was Brought into the Sextons Houfe,
' where prefently he died; and when the
' Sextons Wife, who was then Abroad,
' came home, fhe found the Woman
' Shrouding of the Child, on that other
' end of the Table, where fhe had feen the
' Candle. On a Time my felf and a
' Kinfman coming from our School in
' *England*, and being three or four Hours
' Benighted, e're we could reach home,
' were firft of all Saluted by fuch a *Light*
' or Candle, which coming from a Houfe,
' which we well knew, held his Courfe
' (but not Directly) the High-way to
' Church; fhortly after the Eldeft Son in
' that Houfe Deceafed, and fteered the
' fame Courfe. My felf and my Wife in an
' Evening, faw fuch a Light, or Candle,
' coming to the Church, from her Mid-
' wifes Houfe, and within a Month, fhe
' her felf did follow; at which time my
' Wife did tell me a ftory of her own Mo-
' ther, Mrs. *Catharine Wyat*, an Eminent
' Woman in the Town of *Tenby*, that in
' an Evening being in her Bed-Chamber,
' fhe faw two little Lights juft upon her
' belly, which fhe Affayed to ftrike off with
' her hand, but could not; within a while
' they vanifhed of themfelves. Not long
                                    ' after,

'after, she was Delivered of two Dead-
'born Children: Long sithence there hap-
'pened the like in my own House; but
'to a Neighbours Wife, whom my Wife
'did sometimes call for, to do some work
'or other; and (as I Credibly heard
'within these three days) to some Good
'Gentlewoman also in this very Parish;
'where also not long since, a Neighbours
'Wife of mine, being great with Child,
'and coming in at her own door, met
'two Candles, a Little, and a Big one,
'and within a little after, falling in La-
'bour, she and her Child both Dyed.
'Some Thirty four, or Thirty five years
'bygone, one *Jane Wyat* my Wives Sister;
'being Nurse to Baronet *Rudds* three
'Eldest Children, and (the Lady Mistress
'being Deceased) the Lady Controuler of
'that House going late into a Chamber
'where the Maid Servants Lay, saw there
'no less than five of these Lights together.
'It Happened a while after, the Chamber
'being newly Plaistred, and a Great
'Grate of Coal-fire therein, Kindled to
'Hasten the Drying up of the Plaistring;
'that five of the Maid-Servants went
'there to Bed, as they were wont; but
'(as it fell out) too soon, for in the Morn-
'ing they were all Dead, being Suffocated
'(I conceive) in their Sleep with the
'Steam

steam of the New-Temper'd Lime, and Coal. This was at *Llangathen* in *Caermarthenshire.*

'Some Thirty three or Thirty four
' years ago, upon a *Tuesday* coming towards
home from *Cardigan*, where I had been
enjoyned to Preach the Session-Sermon: *Incipiente adhuc Crepusculo*, and as light as
Noon, and having as yet, Nine long Miles
' to Ride, there seemed twice or thrice
' from behind me, on my right side, and
' between my Shoulder and my Hat, to
' fly a little whitish thing about the bigness of a Walnut, and that *per Intervalla*,
' once in seventy or eighty pace: at first I
' took no notice of it, thinking it had been
' but the glimpsing of my little Ruff, for
' such then I wore, by degrees it waxed
' reddish, and as the night drew on, Redder and redder, at last not *Ignis Fatuus*,
' (for that I partly knew) but *Purus putus*
' *Ignis*, both for Light and Colour. At
' length I turned my Horse twice or thrice
' to see from whence it came, and whether
' it would flash into my face, then nothing
' I could see; but when I turned homewards it flashed as before, until I came
' to a Village called *Llanrislid*, where as
' yet I did not intend to Lodge, though
' there were four Lodgings, and
' one of them (save one) the next House
'in

'in my way, which when I paſſed by
'cloſe, being juſt againſt the door, my Fire
'did flaſh again upon, or very near the
'Threſhold, and there I think it lodged,
'for I ſaw it no more; home ſtill I would
'go, but bethinking my ſelf, that ſo I
'might tempt God, and meet a worſe
'Companion than my former; I turned to
'the fartheſt Lodging in the Town, and
'there after a little reſt, in a brown ſtudy
'becauſe mine Hoſt was an underſtand-
'ing Man, and Literate, and ſuch as
'could, and had but lately read his Neck-
'Verſe in pure Roman Language) I could
'not contain, but muſt needs tell him of
'the Viſion, he the next day to ſome go-
'ing to the Seſſions, they to others there,
'at laſt it came to the Judges ears, inſo-
'much that the greateſt News and Won-
'der at the then Aſſizes was the Preachers
'Viſion. To come at length unto the Pith
'or Kernel (for I have been too long a-
'bout the Husk and Shell) at that very
'Seſſions, one *John William Lloyd*, a Gen-
'tleman who dwelt, and whoſe Son yet
'dwells within a Mile of *Glaſterig*, fell
'Sick, and in his coming homewards, was
'taken with ſuch a violent Paroxiſm, that
'he could Ride no farther than the Houſe,
'where I left my Fire to Entertain him,
'and there he lighted and Lodged, died

P   about

'about four days after. *Ex Abundanti*, 'you shall understand that some Candles 'have been seen to come to my Church 'within these three weeks, and the Corp 'ses not long after.

Mr. *Davis* seems to have been a Learned and Understanding, as well as a Pious Religious *Minister*, and therefore his Testimony must needs carry, with Considerate and thinking Men the more Authority and Force; but now I cannot stay to press it farther. In truth, I have staid so long already on this Head of Argument, and especially on the *Dead Mens Candles*, that nothing can excuse it, but the Rarity and Surprizingness of the Subject. Wherefore I will only desire the *Anti-pneumatist* to Resolve me, *how* these Dead Mens Candles come to be Lighted, and *how* to be directed to go so right from the House of the Person whose Death they do presage, to the Church, or Church-yard where he is to be Lodged, without the influence of Spirits, or some Invisible, but Knowing and Sagacious, ay, Fore-Knowing Beings; I now proceed to the next Argument.

S U B.

SUBS. III.

The Third Argument from Apparitions. Three Stories of them from the Junior Pliny, *in his Epistles. A Recent Story of an Apparition.*

AND the next Argument (the last I will insist upon) to prove the Existence of Spirits, shall be taken from their *Apparition*. By their Apparition, I mean their shewing of themselves to Men in human (or other Animal) shape, and so conversing and dealing with them; I know the word is, and may be taken more largely, but this is the sense I take it in now.

On this Occasion I must mention again the Epistle of *Pliny*, which he sent his Friend *Sura*, to have his Opinion upon this Question, Whether really there were any such things as *Spirits*, that have a Figure of their own, and are a kind of *Numens*; or else, that all are meer fancies, and effects of fear, without any substantial Real Being. *Pliny* himself declares, that he believes their Real Subsistence, and owns he was induced to it by three *Stories*, which he there relates, and I will repeat.

The first is, concerning *Q. Curtius Rufus*, to whom being in *Africk*, where he followed the *Quæstor*, that had that Province assigned to him, there appeared as he was walking alone, a thing in the shape of a Woman of great Beauty, and of a size much larger than ordinary, which told him that he should see the City of *Rome* once again; should bear very honourable Charges; and in fine, return unto *Africk*, with Supream Command, and there die. All which could not but much surprize a Person that was very mean and obscure, (for so was *Q. Curtius* at that time,) and yet says *Pliny*, it came all to pass to a Tittle. He adds, that *Curtius* Sailing to *Carthage*, as soon as he came on shoar the same *Spectre* appeared to him again; and that afterward falling Sick, with a Sickness which none about him thought any any danger of, he remembring what the *Spectre* had told him, and comparing past Events with future, abandon'd all hopes of recovery, and in fine, according to the Prediction of the Apparition, and to his own perswasion, dies in *Africk*. This Story is also in *Tacitus*.

The next is of a Magnificient House in *Athens*, that was Haunted, but in so terrible a manner, that all that dwelt in it died

died with the fright; so it lay void a long time. But at last, a Philosopher called *Athenodorus*, coming to Town, and wanting a House, and seeing an inscription upon this, that it was to be Lett, and for a very low price; he liking the House, and admiring the lowness of the price, inquires, and was fully informed of the Reason. He resolves however to take it, and the rather, for that it was said to be Haunted. Accordingly, in the Evening he orders a Bed to be made for him in the forward part of the House, next the door, and that a Writing-Table, and a 'tile to write with, as also Light should be prepared; which being done, he disposes all his Domesticks in the inner part of the House, and then applies himself to meditation and Writing; by that means imploying both his Thoughts, his Eyes, and his Hands; least otherwise his un-ingaged mind should be possessed of fear, and this impose upon him. While he was thus occupied, all was silent, still, and quiet for a while; but at last he hears at a distance the clattring of Iron, and jingling of Chains, which yet did not so much disturb him, but that, without looking up, he continued his Writing, and incouraged himself all he could. In the mean time, the noise increases, and comes nearer and nearer; first without doors, afterwards within, which makes him look behind him, and then he saw a most terrible *Spectre*, in shape the same as had been represented to him; to wit, a Lean, Meager, Deformed Old Man, with a Long Dangling Beard, his Hair standing an end upon his Head; gives upon his Feet, and Chains in his hands; this Old Gentleman stood still, and seemed to becken with his finger as if he had called to *Athenodorus*. *Athenodorus* answers him the same way with his hand, intimating to him, that he should stay a while, and then goes on writing. But the *Spectre* ratling his Chains over the Philosophers Head, obliges him to look up the second time, when seeing the *Spectre* still beckning as before, he takes up the Light and follows him; who leads the way, but very softly, as one loaded with Fetters; and at last, at a certain place in the *Area* of the House, he Vanishes, and leaves *Athenodorus* alone. *Athenodorus* being thus left, gathers some Herbs and Leaves, and what he could scrape together, and puts them on the place as a mark; and the next day applying himself to the Chief Magistrate, acquaints him with the Story, and advises that the place should be digged, which being done, there were found the Bones of a Man, and Chains,

but

but the Flesh entirely Consumed; they gather the Bones together and bury them, after which the House was Haunted no Longer.

The Two former Stories, tho' they are Related by *Pliny* but upon Tradition, seem very Credible, But the Third, which follows, he tells of his own Knowledge. He had, he says, a Certain Freed man, whose Name was *Marcus*, a Learned Understanding Person. This *Marcus* one Time as he was Lying in Bed with his younger Brother, thought, that he saw something sitting on the same Bed, that, with a Rasor, Shaved his Head all over; and in the Morning it was found, that Really his Head had been Shaved, the Hairs Lying all about the Place. Not Long after says *Pliny*, Another, the Like Accident Hapned, that Confirm'd the Former. For a Certain Youth Lying with many others in the Servants Lodgings, there came unto him through the Window, (for so the Youth Related the Story) two Persons in white Tunicks, who, as he Lay, fell to Shaving of him, and having done it, Returned the same way they came; and that this was a Reall Thing, and not a Dream only, or only a Fancy between Sleeping and Waking, was Manifested (says the Author) by the Day, for when

when this came, it was seen that the Youth was Shaved, and that the Hairs lay Scattered about the Bed.

These are the Instances that Convinced *Pliny*, a Person used to Business, Wise, and Circumspect, not Credulous, or Easie to be Imposed upon, and Abused; to which I will Add but one more, but that shall be a *recent* one, of our own Time, and well Attested: a Story Licensed by a Person of Quality, and of Great worth; who I believe has more Honour than to suffer the World to be Palm'd upon by what He knew a Falsity; and Greater Prudence than to give such a Story a License without some Inquiry after the truth of it. The Story is This,
' The 22 of *February*, 1671, we (says the
' Master that tells it) Sailed from *Graves-*
' *end*; and the 26*th*, by Gods Providence we
' Sailed over the Bar of *Newcastle*, and there
' Loaded the 2d. of *March*. About Nine
' or ten of the Clock in the Night Fol-
' lowing, we having made all clear and
' Ready for the Furtherance of our Voyage,
' some time after Supper I went to Rest,
' when about twelve of the Clock in the
' Night; to the best of my Remembrance,
' I was Awaked out of my Sleep by a
' Great *Noise*, (but saw nothing) which
' to the best of my Capacity bid me *Be gone*,
' and

' and that I had nothing to do there, but
' being so hastily Disturbed, and not cer-
' tain what might be the Cause, I gave it
' over for a *Dream*, and past that Accident
' as Uncertain of the Truth. Now after
' the First Day was Past, about Eight or
' Nine of the Clock at Night I went to
' rest; and about Twelve, my Mate was
' striking a Light to take a Pipe of Tobacco
' (as I suppose) and Expecting the Wherry
' to go up to the Town, being the Tide
' fell out about Two in the Morning, I
' desired the Candle might not be put out,
' and being as well *Awake* as now I am, to
' the best of my Remembrance, I was then
' *Pulled* by the hair of my head off from
' my Pillow, and the *same* words Declared
' unto me as before; and then I *saw* the Per-
' fect Face and Proportion of a *Man*, in a
' Black Hat, Stuff-Coat, and Striped Neck-
' Cloth, with Hanging down hair, and a
' sowre Down-looking Countenance, and
' his Teeth being set in his Head, I had then
' time to say, Lord have Mercy upon me,
' What art? at which he Vanished, yet
' the Candle Burned very Blew, and al-
' most went out: Hereupon being much
' Discontented, I did by the Following
' Post give my owners a just Account of
' what had Befallen me.

' The

'The Fifth of that Instant, we set Sail: about four of the Clock in the Day, the Wind at *W. S. W.* fair Weather, and a Brave Gale off the Shore, which Continued until half an hour after Eleven on *Wednesday* night; at which time the Man at the Helm called out that he could not *stir* the Helm: but after I had pulled off the Whip-staff; the Ship steered as before, being still fair Weather, the Wind then coming to the *N. W.* and Snowing Weather, but very fair and clear. I was yet Doubtful of more Wind; and therefore caused the Men to furl the Fore Top-sail, and Lower down the Main Topsail upon the back of the Main sail, but could not with all the strength we had hale in; the Weather brake off the fore Top-sail, when this was still in my Judgment, that our Ship did hale as much, as when our sails were out, then we haled up our Main-sail, and still the Ship had the same Lift as with a Large Wind, which to my Judgment might be half a streak, or thereabouts.

'By This time it was Two of the Clock, then our Men tried the Pump, and found Little or no Water in her: the Man at the Helm called out, that the *Candle* Burned so Blew in the Lanthorn;

' thorn; that it gave Little or no Light,
' and three several times went out, so that
' I held the Candle to the Look-out, which
' Candle did burn very well, and shewed
' a good Light, but of a sudden our Ship
' would not feel the Helm so kindly as
' before, and brought all our Sails Aback,
' then our Ship heeled as much to Wind-
' ward, as before to Leeward: the Glass
' being out, we went to the Pump, and
' found no Water in the Ship, but she
' did not steer well, Neither could I find
' the Reason, being still so fair Weather,
' this unkind steerage made me Urgent
' to try the Pump yet more, but I could
' not get the upper Box to work, nor
' stir, but having taken that up, and try-
' ing with the Pump-hook, we could not
' come near the Lower Box by a foot and
' half, which to my Judgment was Hin-
' dred by something like a *Bull-fish* or
' Woolsack, that as we forced down, gave
' up again with the Hook: Whereupon
' Mistrusting that all was not well, I
' caused our Men to keep the Coat of our
' Pump up; and my self Loosned the Tack;
' in the mean time I ordered two Men to
' Loose the Boat, which they did being
' Lashed in three Places: yet they do not
' Remember to this hour, that they Loos-
' ned any of them but the Middlemost;

' and

' and with three Men in her, the Boat
' *went over* the Top of the Foresheet,
' which lay above the stem, without
' Touching it, with such Violence, as
' even Amazed us that saw it; And they
' that were in the Boat, gave such loud
' cryes, as frighted him at the Helm, who
' came Running out unknown to me, but
' finding the Ship coming nearer the Wind
' then formerly, I Ran to the Stair-case,
' to bid him put the Helm over, but
' could not : and hearing one jump down
' at the Hatch, which was open at the
' half-deck, did suppose that the Helms-
' man came Down again; and calling him
' by his Name to come and help me, the
' word was no sooner out of my Mouth.
' but I Perceived the *same* Person that I
' had formerly seen before we came out of
' the Harbour; who came violently to
' me, saying, be gone, you have no more
' to do here. Throwing me in at the
' Cabbin door, clear upon the Top of
' the Table; When I crying out, In the
' Name of God what art, he *Vanished*
' away in a Flash of Fire; thinking withal
' that the Ship had split in a Thousand
' pieces, it giving such a Crack. The Men
' thereupon calling out, Master, if you be
' a Man come away, did something Re-
' vive me, and striving to have got to my
       ' Chest

'Cheft, being I had got fome Money in
' it, I found that fomething Hindred me,
' but what it was I could not tell. Then
' Perceiving the Main Sea coming in fo
' Faft, that I was up to the waft, before
' I could get out of the Cabbin, and find-
' ing all our Men in the Boat but only
' one, I defired him to get a Compafs;
' which he did, yet could never after
' know what became of it. We were no
' fooner in the Boat, but the Ship Sank
' Down, and yet having a Great Sea Fur
' Gown, which lay upon the Dicker, up-
' on the Ships going Down, the very up-
' fet of the Water brought it to the Boats
' fide, and one of our Men took it in, we
' Reckoned our felves to be Ten or Twelve
' Leagues *E. S. E.* from the *Spern*, I Per-
' ceived the Fane at the Main-top-Maft-
' Head, when the Ship was funk: we
' Continued in the Boat from three in the
' Morning till ten or eleven that day,
' when we were taken up by a *Whitby*
' Ketch, who ufed us very Kindly, and
' towed our Boat at his Stern with two
' Ends of a Haufer, till fhe brake away:
' She being Bound for *Newcaftle*, and the
' Wind being Contrary, did on the *Satur-*
' *day* Following, fet us a Shore at *Grimsby*
' in *Hull* River, where the Mayor gave us
' a Pafs for *London*. This is a True and
' Perfect

'Perfect Relation to the best of my know-
'ledge in every Respect. *John Pye* Master.
'And Attested by *Nine* Men more all Be-
'longing to my Ship.

'I Had forgot to Express, that one side
'of my Face is Burnt and Blasted sorely,
'which I felt within half an hour after I
'was gone out of the Ship; but how it
'came upon me in the Ship I could not
'tell being then in a Great Horror and
'Amazement. Thus *John Pye*.

This seems an Undeniable Evidence of the Reality of Apparitions.

SECT. III.

The Apparition of Spirits twofold, Real, or Visional; both ways Explained. A Conceit about the Appearing of Ghosts Rejected. That most Apparitions of Spirits are Visional, not Real, Evinced by several Considerations. Some Phænomena *of Apparitions Salved. Of the Distribution of Spirits.*

THIS Last Argument for the Real Existence of Spirits taken from their Apparition, Invites me to Consider the *Ways* in which they use to Appear. And There are *two* ways in which they do, or may *Appear*, the one Real, the other I call Visional.

I call it *Real* Appearing, when they present themselves to some of the Outward senses, and (particularly to the Eye,) in some thing that does Really Affect it; and so, by means of the sense, (in the same way as all Corporeal External *Objects* do) they Affect and stir the *Imagination*. I call their Appearing *Visional*, when by Affecting or Stiring the *Imagination*, they occasion such Appearances as seem External to the *Eye*, or other *senses*, tho'

tho' indeed there is nothing that does really affect *it*, or *them*, from without. This Conception is grounded upon comon Obfervation. For few are ignorant that things appear as external to the fenfe, *not only* when impreffions are made upon it from without, by real Objects that move it, *but alfo* when the imagination is fmartly ftricken by fomething from within, for fo it is in *Dreams*, in which all things do feem as really tranfacted for the time; (and not feldom, where the impreffion is very ftrong, even after that men are awakened) as when the External Senfe is affected by Objects.

Well then, in real Apparitions of Spirits, the external fenfe is immediately afaffected; but in thofe that are Vifional, the Imagination.

The real appearing of Spirits is genenerally thought to be performed, *either* by their affuming of Bodies that are already prepared; *or* by Figuring the Air, or fome other Elementary Subftance into the fhapes in which they appear; which latter is done by the *Plaftic* Power of the Imagination; a Power a Spirit is believed to have, becaufe we truly experience *fuch an one* in our incorporated felves, not only upon the *Spirits* in the Brain, which are *Figured* into a Thoufand fhapes at our pleafure, pleasure, in the several things we do imagine; but in some cases, upon external Bodies; as in the *Signatures* of *the Fœtus*; not to mention other less certain, but strongly asserted instances.

And indeed, I take the former *Thought* in this Matter, for a much more *probable* one, than that of some others; which is, that Spirits do appear by Condensation of their *Vehicles*, and disappear by Attenuating them; this being not a very easie Conception, for of what Matter must such Vehicles consist? ay, of *what* vast *Extension* must the Vehicle of a Spirit be, in its own proportion? if when it is Condensed and Shrunk so much, as it must to become an Object of Sense, it is yet in *Dimension* Equal, and sometimes Superiour, unto *that* of a Man.

Some are of the Opinion, that *Ghosts* (by which I mean the Apparitions of Souls Departed) do for the most part by virtue of their Formative *Plastic* Power, frame unto themselves the Vehicles in which they appear, out of the *Moisture* of their own deserted Bodies; this being a Matter that is believed more Congenial to them, and more Sympathetical; and for that Reason, they say, it is, that Ghosts do often appear in *Church-Yards*; and that they do not appear but *for some short time*, to wit, before the moisture is wholly dried up; as also, that the Ancients used to *Burn* not to *Burie* the Dead; for *Cardan* tells us, that during that Custom, there was no such Appearing of Ghosts as is now.

But this Opinion has very little ground; for besides, that it does account but for the Apparition of *Souls*, and not that of *Angels*, good, or bad; tho' it is very probable that Departed Souls, if at any time they appear, they do it the same way that Angels are used to do, since there is the same reason they should. I say besides this, it is certain (if any Stories of such a nature are certain) that pretended Ghosts have appeared so long after their decease from their several Bodies, that nothing could remain of these but the Dust; and it is also certain, that many Persons have been *seen* (to all Appearances) while alive, in their proper Shapes and Meen, and with the very Cloaths they were used to wear; and this could not be done by means of Vehicles framed of their Radical moisture. In truth, this last is a very cross *Phænomenon*; a *Phænomenon* that renders all Apparition of Ghosts uncertain and questionable, since it seems to infer, that it is not the Departed Soul it self that appears, whenever there is such an Appari-

Apparition, but some other Spirit that *Personates* it.

For my own part, I see many Difficulties in the way, of the real Apparition of Spirits; for besides that of the *assuming* of Bodies, many times they do Eat and Drink, and perform several other *Vital Actions*, that seem very hard to be accounted for in that way; so that I am much inclined to believe, (that) their Apparition is mostly, if not only *Visional*; not by an immediate affection of the External Sense, but by affecting and striking the Imagination in the way I have mentioned before. And herein I am confirm'd, in that it seems to have been the common Sentiment of all the Ancients; who did for this reason (as I noted before) call the *Apparitions* of Spirits *Phantasmata*, or *Idola*; to wit, because they were rather *Imaginative*, than *Real*, not as Mr. *Hobbs* would carry it, as if they thought that all Spirits were only *Phantasmata*, or meer Fancies, but because they thought that Spirits used not to *Appear* but by affecting and striking the Fancy. And this is Evident, in that they did call Apparitions not only *Phantasmata*, or Images, but also *Pneumata* or Spirits; by the latter Expression signifying the *nature* of the things that did appear, as by the former, the *way* in which

which they appeared. Thus *Luke*, when he would intimate that the Disciples (at the time they saw our Lord after his Resurrection) supposed that they had seen a Spirit, does not use the word *Phantasma*, as the two other Evangelists, *Matthew*, and *Mark*, do, on the like occasion, but the word *Pneuma*, Luke 24. 37. *But they [the Disciples] were terified and frighted, and supposed they had seen a Spirit.* [πνεῦμα.] I add, that from the *different* Expressions that these Evangelists do use, on the like occasion; *Matthew* and *Mark* expressing the supposed seeing of a Spirit, by seeing of a *Phantasm*, [φάντασμα,] but *Luke*, by seeing of a *Spirit*; [πνεῦμα,] one may infer, that when they thought the Apparition to be of a *Good Spirit*, they called it πνεῦμα, or a *Spirit*; but when of a *Bad*, they called it *Phantasma*, as who would say, a *Sprite*, an Hob-Goblin, an illusion of Devils; without conceiveing, what perhaps some others will judge as propable, that they had an Opinion (as, if I do not mis-remember, the Modern *Platonists* had,) that *Good* Spirits did use to appear *really*, but *bad* ones, by disturbing and *troubling the Fancy*.

Another Consideration that induces me to think the Apparition of Spirits to be mostly (if not always) Visional, is, that all

all *Appearance* will be the same in this business of Apparitions, upon the *Hypothesis* that they are but Visional, as upon that, that they are real; since *Common Dreams*, in those that sleep; and *waking ones* in the Melancholy, the Maniacal, and the Hysterical, do seem as real to them, as any things that are most so. And as *some* Appearances will equally as well be salved upon one *Hypothesis* as upon the other, so there are *others*, that will be better salved upon the Visional, than on the Real Hypothesis; particularly this, that *Spectres* are often said to be seen by one Person in a Room, that are not by others in the same Room, tho' they look where they are said to be seen. A Spirit may be easily Conceived to affect and strike the *Imagination* of one Person, without doing so to anothers; but that the same *External Object* should be seen by one, and not by another that has the same advantage, is somewhat harder to think, and I had almost said, cannot be conceived without a double Miracle. In short, one can better conceive how Spirits should eat, and drink, &c. in the Visional, than in the Real Hypothesis.

I know it may be told me, that it is more usual for Spirits to appear by *Night* than by *Day*, and in *Dark* and Gloomy places,

places, than in open and lightsome; and those who hold the real apparition of Spirits, will think that they can give a better account of this *Phænomenon*, than others can, who do believe it but Visional. For they will say; *Those* of them that do hold the Opinion of a Spirits appearing by *Condensation* of his own Vehicle, that the *Cold* of the Night, as also of umbragious and gloomy places, where the Sun does not enter, or of solitary uninhabited ones, where Fire is not used, does much contribute to the Conspissation of the Spirits Vehicle: And *Those* that hold the Opinion that Spirits appear *by Forming* to themselves a Body of Air, will say, that the Spissitude of the Air, which is greater by Night than by Day (when the presence of the Sun attenuates it,) and greater in gloomy and uninhabited, than in lightsom and inhabited places, does make the Formation of a Body (and by consequence their Apparition) more agreeable and easie to them. But what can be said of this appearance in the *Visional* Hypothesis.

I cannot foresee how very acceptable, or otherwise, such a Discourse as this will be unto others, but to me it is of an Aspect (that is) not very Agreeable. For that the *Angelical Vehicle* should be obnoxious to the impressions of Heat and Cold,

(as

(as is in the *First* Opinion,) seems somewhat a gross Conception; nor can I see how the Spissitude, or the Tenuity of the Air should signifie much, either to further or to hinder the making a body of Air by a Spirit, (as it is apprehended to do in the *second* Opinion,) if a Spirit be conceived (as he must) to work *Magically*, and not *Mecannically*, in it. But not to insist on this, but to answer directly. The Reason then why Spirits do appear in the Night rather than in the Day, and in dark gloomy solitary places rather than in others, is from the *silence* and vacancy that is at such times, and in such places, so that the Imagination not being possessed, or diverted, by External Objects, is more attentive unto, and Consequently more susceptive of internal impressions; there being the same Reason for *this* Phænomenon, as there is for some *others*, to wit, our better hearing a Sound by Night than in the Day, and our seeing of the Images in a Darkned Room upon a Paper, or Wall, that Disappear as soon as a greater Light is admitted.

By these and other Considerations, I am more inclined to a belief of the *Visional*, than of the *Real* Apparition of Spirits; the *Former* being accompanied with fewer Difficulties, and also being a thing that is

easily

easily conceived; for one that thinks, will more easily admit an Angel can affect and stir the imagination, (which we see both many *Distempers*, and more *Meats* and *Drinks* can do;) than that it should *Create* a Body, or assume one Created; or in fine, be able to alter its own Vehicle, so much from its proper *Dimension*, that the squeezing of an Elephant into that of a Mouse, is of no Comparison with it.

I confess, I should be more inclined than I am to the *Real Hypothesis*, if I could believe the *Spagirical Resurrection* of Plants, or the *Reality* of Apparitions resembling Men, that are said to be seen in Distilling-Vessels, upon the Distillation of Human Blood; of which *Peter Borellus* (a Curious, but too Credulous Author) tells us in his Observations, *Cent.* 4. *Obs.* 62. I fear, with more presumption, than certainty. For my part, I must acknowledge my unbelief as to it.

I will only add, for the fuller clearing of the Theory of the Apparition of *Spirits*, that what *Gravity* or weight is in respect of Elementary Bodies, That a strong *Inclination* or *Habit*, and *Will* or Passion is unto Souls; and Consequently, that we seldom hear of the Apparition of *Any* but of such as went out of the Body with great *Reluctance*; with a violent Passion

sion of *Revenge*; or with a strong *Desire* of having something done, that was in their will, but not in their power. And of the appearing of *such* we often hear; but *whether* the Apparition is of the Departed *Soul* it self, or of its *Representative* only, to wit, some *Genius Personating* the Deceased; and *why* (often times) it appears unto Persons no way concerned, and not to those that are, when it would have something revealed; as *also* the Laws of the Spiritual World, (for Laws there must be, which do confine and regulate the motions of Spirits;) these, and many other points in the business of Spirits are all unknown unto me, and perhaps are only known unto God.

I should now proceed to the *Distribution* of Spirits; but this entirely depends upon the History of them, and we know but little of that History: Besides, there is in what we are thought to know, so much of Tale, Romance, and Invention, that, upon strict inquiry, not one Relation of a hundred holds true, even of their Apparitions; an Observation which obliged *Lucian* of old, and *many* now, to Ridicule them all. Wherefore I resolve to Omit, as a Task too hard for me, to discourse of their *Kinds*, and their *Orders*; only in

General,

General, I will adventure to affirm (if this be to Adventure, to say, what few will deny,) that that there are several *Species* ; Angels in *Heaven*, and Devils out of it; and perhaps a *Lower sort* of Spirits than those we commonly call Devils. But for the *Celestial Hierarchy,* as *Dionysius* (the True, or the False) has set it out, and the *Distinction* in it, that he makes of *Seraphim,* of *Cherubim,* of *Thrones,* of *Dominations,* of *Vertues,* of *Powers,* of *Principalities,* of *Arch-Angels,* and of *Angels* ; as also of the Politick *Government* of *Devils,* and the several *Orders* that are in *it* : One had need be a Saint, and as illuminated with Revelation as *Dionysius* himself was, to understand the *Former* ; and for the *Latter,* he must be a Conjurer of the Highest Class, and possibly more than a Conjurer, to have any, or any certain Account of it. One that is Curious may find many, and very strange, things upon this Subject in *Cardan,* in his Books, *de varietate,* and *de subtilitate*; and in *Cornelius Agrippa,* in his, of Occult Philosophy, *L.* 1. *C.* 11. *Fernelius* also has something, which he has gathered out of *Plato,* and others, concerning the

Kinds

Kinds of Spirits, in his Treatise *De Abditis rerum Causis*, L. 1. C. 11. but all is but Guess and Conjecture. See *Gaspar Schottus* his *Physica Curiosa*, L. 1. C. 12. &c.

CHAP.

CHAP. VIII.

Another Essay about the Nature of Animals and Spirits.

SECT. I.

The Subject farther Illustrated, by a Comparison of the Universe with a particular Animal. The Universe a whole; Particular Animals but Members of that whole. A Particular Animal is as an Organ with its faculty; the Universe, as a Body composed of several Organs, with a Soul that endues these Organs with several Faculties. A Demonstration even to sense, of a common Principle that penetrates throughout the Universe. In what sense a Soul is a faculty, and in what a Principle of Faculties. Two senses of the word Soul, and how in both, it may be conceived as a Principle of Faculties. The Soul in its state of separation becomes a Spirit properly. Soul is the name of a part, a Spirit the name of a whole Substance. God the Central Sun, and Fountain of all Souls and Spirits. The Emanation of Souls and Spirits from God, or from his Spirit, set out in the Comparison of Light and Colours. Not only Philosophers, and Poets, but even many Christian Doctors, and particularly St. Augustin, compared God in respect of his influence in and over the Universe, unto the Soul in a Man.

IN

IN the Precedent Chapter, I have offered to my Reader something concerning the nature of *Animals*, as well those that are Invisible, called *Spirits*, as those that are Visible; but the subject being Obscure, I think my self obliged to turn it every way, to see what further Light may be Given to it; and therefore I will now Enlarge upon *one Point*, in Relation unto it, that I did but touch before, whereby I hope to Illustrate it.

It is Received on all hands, except by *Cartesians*, that in every visible *Animal*, as well as in *Man*, there is a Body Composed of several Organs, and there are several Faculties or Powers, according to the several Organs; and there is a Common Principle (called a Soul) that Permeating throughout the Body, doth Furnish it in its several Organs with those several Faculties.

Now, As all the *Organs* of any Particular Animal, tho' being Compared *one with Another*, they are *several*, not Parts one of Another, but a kind of wholes, and have their several Faculties; yet in respect of the *Body*, they are but *Parts*, and all Influenced by a *Common Principle*, which giveth being to *its* several Faculties, but is none of them it self. Why may not all

all the *Animals*, themselves (as well the Invisible as the Visible,) that do Exist in the *Universe*, be, in respect of *this* but as so many *Parts*, so many Organs. (some more Simple, others more Compound) Actuated by some *Common Principle* that Penetrates throughout *it*; and yet, in Respect *one of Another*, be several *wholes*, that have their several Powers and Faculties? And then, *as* all the Particular Animals would, in truth, be but as so many several Organs Endued with several Faculties, in which the Organ or System of Organs would be the *Body*, the Faculty or System of Faculties the *Soul*; *so* all of them taken together, would be an Entire Body [of the *Universe*] Actuated by an Universal Principle, (as by a Common Soul) that should Endow it with those several Powers and Faculties. In short; why may not the Universe Really be Body and Soul, and every Particular Animal (as a part thereof) be Organ and Faculty, in the same sense that in our ordinary Common way of Conceiving, every Particular Animal is Body and Soul, and the Parts of it, Organs and Faculties? But to Proceed.

This is Certain, that what in Animals, and particularly in a Man, we do Commonly

monly call a *Faculty*, is neither that which commonly is called the Soul, nor is it meerly the Body, or any Part of the Body, but a *Result*; some Third thing Arising from them both in Conjunction. For the *Eye*, for Example, tho' never so well Qualified, doth not see, unless the Mind or Soul do Attend; and again, the *mind* or Soul, tho' never so Attentive, cannot see, unless it has the use of an Eye, to see with; so that the *Power* of seeing neither is in the Eye barely, nor in the Soul barely, but belongs to the *Animal*, which is Soul and Body: as arising from the presence of the Soul in such a Particular Part, or Organ, of the Body. And the like is to be said of other Powers.

And yet if all the Faculties that are united in Man, were supposed *Separated* each from other, *with* their several Organs, and so to be in the Nature of *wholes*, and this without the supposal of any Thing else; for Example, that the *Eye* could see apart, the *Ear* hear apart, and the *Tongue* taste apart from the Body; there would, to all Appearance, be so *many* several Animals, and Consequently so many several Souls: So that what is called a *Faculty* only, while it is in a part, is Denominated a *Soul*, in the whole; and then, where the Body is a Compage, or System

of

of Organs, the Soul must be a *System* of Faculties: and yet be *one* still, in the same sense as the Body is.

But here I must expect it *shall be told* me, that the True and commonly Received Notion of a Soul is, that it is the *Principle* of the Faculties called Vital and Animal, and not any one of them it self, or any System of them All: To which I *Answer*, that this is indeed the *Popular* and Common Notion, but how true it is, and how much Adjusted to the Nature of the Soul, cannot be understood but by making some Distinction in the sense of word [Soul.]

The word [Soul] may be taken *Two ways*, the one of which I will call the *Philosophical*, the other the *Popular* sense of the Word.

First then, word [Soul] may be taken *Philosophically*, as a Name of *all* the Causes together, that are necessary for the Producing of Vital and Animal Actions, in the several Species of Animals: and so, tho' it is commonly considered as if it were some *Substantial thing*, that Differ'd from them All, yet *indeed* it is nothing but a *Modification* of their Action, as they are All in Conjunction. And *Dicearchus*, who Affirmed there was no

such

such thing as a Soul, if he meant but thus, was very Excusable; for in this sense, a Soul is nothing but a *Result*, that is, a *Mode of Conceiving* (for this I mean by Result) of all the *Causes* that must be Joyned for Animal, or Vital Actions, as *they* do either *Qualifie*, or else *Aid*, each others Influence. And in this sense, as a *Soul*, in respect of the *Action*, of a Particular Organ, may be called a *Faculty*; so in respect of the whole *Body*, a *Soul*, is a *System* of Faculties. Thus *Life* in Animals, arises from the Concurrence of many things; which things therefore, in that *Concurrence*, as they are the *Prince* of Life, so they may be called the *Soul*; [for by *Soul*, is meant nothing, but the Principle of that, we call the Life;] if one of these is wanting (that are necessary,) the Life ceases, and we say, the Soul is *gone*; but then again, (supposing all the other Requisites Remaining as they ought to be, and Ready to do their Parts,) if that *one*, which was wanting is Restored, there is again a Concurrence of *all* the Causes Requisite to Life, and so, with the Life, the Soul is said to *Return*, or come again. For Example, there is in Snakes, in Dormice, in Swallows, and in other *Dormitive Creatures* of that kind, and (if we

shall

shall believe *Guagninus*, *apud Schottum*, Phyſ. Curioſ. *l.* 1. *part.* 2. *C.* 38. §. 4.) in some *Men* too, (for so he says of the Inhabitants of *Lucomoria*, a certain Country of *Ruſſia*, that there is) an Actual Suspension of the Exercise of Life in all the Species of it during Winter, while their Spirits lie Congealed and un-active; so that tho' all the Organs of those Animals, in other Respects, are duly Qualified and Disposed, yet there being not, for that season, sufficient Heat Imparted to them from the Sun, to put their *Spirits* in Motion, *These*, like *Mercury* while Cold, are wholly un-active, and so for several Months there is a Cessation of Life (for Life is a Sort of Action) in all the sensible Instances of it. But then again on the other side, nothing being wanting but a due *Heat*, (as unto *Mercury*, to put it in Actual Motion,) as soon as the Sun Returns, and with its warmth, Communicates that Motion that is Requisite to the Spirits, and other Parts, for the Invigorating, and the stirring of them, there Results that Action, or Exercise of Organs, which *we* call *Life*, and which in many Places of Holy *Scripture*, is called the *Soul*. tho' *commonly* we call the Soul the *Principle*, not the *Exercise* of Life; but then by a Principle we must mean the Concourse of all the Requisite Causes,

Causes, and so the Soul in Effect will be but a *Faculty*, or rather a System of Faculties. And so much for the *Philosophical Sense* of the Word Soul.

But besides the *Former*, there is Another meaning of the word [Soul], which I call the *Popular*, because it is the most usual, and that is, when it is Taken not for *all* the Causes together, or the Result of them, as in the Former, but for the *Principal* and Chief Cause of Animal and Vital Actions, which in the Holy Scriptures is called the *Spirit*; [*who knoweth the Spirit of a Man that goeth Upward, or the Spirit of a Beast that goeth Downward?*] And so when a Person dies, he is said to to give up his Spirit, to Give up the Ghost.

And thus a Soul may be Conceived, a System of very subtle Refined *Matter*, such as *Light*, (but in some more, in others less Refined) that gives the last Disposition to a Body and its Organs for the receiveing of Vital *Cogitative Influence*, from the Original Mind; it is the *Texture* and Qualification of the *Body*, and the Organs that compose it, that is the Ligament and *Bond* of union between this subtle Matter or Spirit, and *That*; but it is the *Subtle Matter* or Spirit that is the *Vinculum* or Bond of Union between the Body and the *Original Mind*.

In this way of Conceiving; This System of Subtle Matter while it is in the Body, tho' it is called a *Spirit*, becaufe of its fubtlety, in truth, may be but a *Soul*, that is, a *Means* only of Conveying the Vital Influence into the Body, from the Original Mind; but then again, out of the Body, as the Syftem of it may be, it may become a *Spirit* properly fo called; it being then no longer a Part, (as a Soul muft (be), which is only a Mediate Subject,) but a whole, and fo a Terminative Subject, of the Influence of the Original Mind: in fhort, it becomes a *Suppofitum* or Subfiftent by it felf. That the Soul is but a Mediate Subject while it is in the Body, and not a Terminative, fo that properly the *Animal*, (which is Soul and Body,) and not the Soul only, is Agent in all that Paffes, feems Probable, in that all the Ordinary *Actions* of the Man, that commonly are faid to be the Souls, are plainly *Organical*; nothing can be Inftanced in, as Proceeding from the Soul while it is in the Body, that is not properly *Animal*: even *Intellection* it felf, is not an Action only of the Soul, or *Anima*, but (as the *Latins* would Exprefs it,) an Action of the *Animus* or Underftanding; *which* is to be Conceived as an Animal and Organical Faculty, that is, as a thing arifing rising Principally, but not only, from the Soul: for so does *Cotta* Distinguish, *apud Cicerol.* 3. *de nat. Deor.* when he says, *Probabilius videtur tale quiddam esse* Animum, *ut sit ex Igne, atque Anima temperatum.*

It is true, the *Ordinary* way of Conceiving is much *otherwise*, for the *Soul* is Considered by the *Most*, as if it were an *Angel* or Spirit, that only dwelt in the Body as in a House; and thus the Soul is the *man*, the Body but as a *Tabernacle*, or a Garment to it: nor is this a meer *Platonical* Notion; it is Conformable to the way of *speaking* in the Holy Scriptures; as, where St. *Paul* says, *I Desire to be Dissolved, and to be with Christ*; Also, where he tells the Corinthians, *we know if our Earthly House of this Tabernacle were Dissolved*, &c. And for certain, if the Theory of the *Pre-existence* of Souls is a True one, this Opinion is beyond dispute. However, I will not Determine in this matter, since the Language of the Scripture is often Adapted but to the Conceptions of the Vulgar, and therefore cannot be the Standard of Philosophical Truth; and it is certain, that even in our Saviours time a many *Pythagorean* and *Platonical Doctrines*, and *this* in particular of the Pre-existence of Souls, and the Souls being the Man, had obtained to be Vulgar among the *Jews*; As appears by

that

that Question of the *Disciples*, which they put to our Lord, *was this Man* Born *Blind for his own*; or for *his Parents sin?* for it suppofes, that the Man might fin, and therefore also suppofes that he *was*, before he was Born, for he could not Sin, if he was not (in Being.) Besides, the *Genesis* or way of Generation of Animals, seems to Favour the former opinion more than the latter; for in the latter Opinion, the Soul is conceived as an *Assistant*, rather than an Informing *Form*, and so rather as an *Animal*, than as a *Part* of one: which doth not so well consist with the Method of Generation. In fine, the Distinction between *Souls* and *Abstract Spirits*, as to their Natures, cannot be set out with that Distinctness and clearness in the Latter, as in the Former Opinion.

But Take it either way; if we Distinguish *Soul* and *Faculties*, and do hold, that Animal *Actions* are the Effects of Faculties, but that the Soul is the Principal cause of those Faculties; why may it not be Affirmed (as I Hinted before) that the *Mosaical Spirit* is, unto all the *Bodies* in the Universe, (those of Invinsible, as well as of Visible Animals) what the Soul Conceived of, after this manner, is in our selves unto *ours*? So that All particular Animals in respect of the Universe, should be be but as the several Organs in any Particular Animal; and then Particular *Souls* should be but as so many *Portions of the subtle Matter*, through which, and by means of which, the *Mosaical* Spirit (as a *Soul of the Universe*) should Radiate into the several Bodies, and give them their *Faculties*. In short, we may conceive particular Souls as so many *Animi* (for now I Distinguish, as *Cotta* do's, between *Animus* and *Anima*;) and that the *Anima*, that is the Sourse of All these *Animi*, is but one, throughout the Universe. Why may not this be so? And if it may, it must, since then, the being of Subordinate *Anima* (other than *Animi*) would be superfluous and unnecessary; and Beings are not to be Multiplied but on Necessity.

Besides, there is Reason to think there is but *one Soul* Diffus'd throughout the Universe, if it be Allowable to make the same Judgment in Reference to the whole, that, upon good Considerations, may be Framed of the Parts which come Distinctly within our View. For in this *Terrestrial World*, as to the several *Regions* of it, the Animal, the Vegetable, and the Mineral, it is as certain, that all had but one *Plastic*, as that the Body of a Man, or any other particular Animal, had not

more

more. The Evidence is the same for Both. There is a sensible *Analogy* and Correspondence in *Fabric* and Conformation, not only between the several *Species* of *Animals*, (which is very manifest in *Comparative Anatomy*); but also, in a good degree, between *Plants* and *Animals*, and *Minerals* and *Plants*. Again, there is a like *Connexion* between the *Beings* that fill those several Regions, as there is between the *Parts* that compose particular Animals; There are no *Vacuities*, or Gaps in *Nature*, in respect of *Species*, no Jumps or Leaps, but all in orderly *Gradation :* Extreams are Knit and United by *Participles* that partake of Both; and all is *full*, without any Chasms. Thus (to touch it in an Example) *Minerals* and *Vegetables* are Joyned by *Lithodendra* or Stone-Plants, such as Coral and the like; *Vegetables* and *Animals* by *Zoophytes* or Plantanimals, such as the sensible Plant, the Scythian Lamb, and the like. And in the *General Kinds* of Animals, between *Fowls* and *Beasts*, the *Bat*; Between *Fishes* and *Fowls*, the *Flying Fish*; between *Terrestrial* and *Aquatic* Animals, those that are called *Amphibious*, are Middle *Uniting Species*, &c. Farther, there is a *Conformity* in their *Origination*, as well as in their Structure and Fabrick; for Plants as well as Animals are Produced

by

by *Semination*; and even Minerals and Mettals have their *Matrices*; and tho' they have not what is properly called *Seed*, they have something that is Analogous in their Production. In fine, the *Transmutation* of things, and the Easie Transition of them from one Region unto Another, evinces it. The *Transmutation* of Earthly and Aqueous Bodies into *Vegetables*, is so Obvious, as I need not to Instance; *That* of Vegetables into *Animal Concretes* is as certain, tho' not so Obvious and Usual. The Animation of *Horse-hairs* that fall into Pools in the Summer time, may be an Example; but those are more Adequate, that are Given in the Generation of *Barnacles*; and in the Animation of the Branches of certain *Trees*. I Vouch not these Instances upon uncertain Report (tho' some will believe it no other,) but on the credit of a Person Grave and Unsuspected, I mean the Excellent *Schottus*, who in his *Physica Curiosa*, l. 1 C. 20. among other Examples very pertinent to this purpose, relates those I have mentioned, on his own Knowledge. *Pili,* (says he, *è caudis equorum in aquam pluviam, fossis ac scrobibus exceptam decidentes Animantur, & in graciles ac Longos vermes instar Serpentum convertuntur, ut ipsemet non semel vidi. Aves Anatum formâ ex Ramis Arborum deciduis intra aquas in Scotiâ*

Scotiâ & Hebridibus Infulis nafci teftantur multi Scriptores; Ipfemet vidi Ramorum extremitates paulatim animâ fenfitiva Informatas decidiſſo & Avolaſſe.

Now, ſo much *Uniformity* even in difformity; ſuch *Connexion*; and ſo Eaſie *Tranſition* from one Region into Another, cannot be conceived to be in the World, without conceiving at the ſame time, that as it had but *one Author* or common Plaſtic at firſt; ſo ſtill it has but *one Principle*, that hath the ordering, the Diſpoſing the Framing and Actuating of it, in all its Parts.

But to make it more Conceivable, that *all* Particular Beings may be Animated by but *One*, and yet being ſuch Diverſity as they are, let us conſider that Glorious thing we call *Light*, which as it Proceeds and Iſſues from the Sun, is of *one* Nature, but meeting with divers *Objects*, and Receiving Different *Modifications*, according to thoſe of the Objects it meets with, is varied into a *Thouſand Colours*, of Different Natures from the Light, as well as one from Another. And it is even thus with the *Vital Energy*, or Light that flows from God (the Intellectual *Sun* and Father of Spirits,) for *This*, tho' as it Proceeds and flows from him, it is but of one Nature, yet, according to the Bodies it meets with,

(it)

(it) becomes Diversified and Varied, into a Thousand shall I say? or rather into Infinite *Faculties* and Powers, that, in their particular Natures, are as Different from the Original Vital Energy it self, (taken in it self.) as All are one from Another. In short, the first Subject of Vital Energy is the *Mosaical Spirit*; but This, as it is Received in Bodies of several Fabricks, Dispositions and Textures, (as well in Visible, as in Invisible Animals, become *Diversified* into several Powers and Faculties; or (which is the same in Effect,) becomes in *Each* a *Principle* of Actions that Differ one from Another, as much as the *Bodies* do that Invest it, and as the *Motions*, that, by means of those Bodies, do Affect and Modifie it. Modifications of the Cogitative Faculties, or of the Immediate Principle that makes the Being Cogitative, are called *Ideas*, or *Images*, and are the same unto the Mind, in the *Sense*, and the *Understanding*, that Sensible *Species* (as they commonly are called) are unto the Light in the Air: for as *These* are nothing but Modification of the Light, so *Those* are of the Mind.

SECT.

SECT. II.

Several Objections against the Former Hypothesis considered, First, that it makes Souls to be Faculties or Powers, whereas indeed they are Actions, or Acts. This Objection Answered, and the notion of the Souls being a Principle and Faculty, rather than an Action, cleared. The Second Objection, that in this Hypothesis the Deity is considered as an Immanent, and not (what he is) as a Transient cause of all things, Removed; and how he is both the one and the other, shewed, and Confirmed by the Authority of St. Austin, and other Christian Fathers; as well as of the Chiefest Philosophers. The Third Objection, that hereby God and Nature are Confounded; Answered, by shewing how God and Nature are Distinguished in this Hypothesis. The Last and strongest Objection, that if there were but one Original Perceptive Principle throughout the Universe, all Animals would have the same Perceptions, which they have not. This Objection Removed, and the Reason of Different Perceptions in Different Animals cleared.

THO' I have Endeavoured to Anticipate Objections in the Discourse that I have made, all along as I made it, yet, to give them a farther clearing, and thereby elucidate more fully the *Hypothesis* that I Espouse, this Section shall be Employed in proposing in express Terms, such *Objections* as do lye against it, and in giving them the necessary Answers.

The First *Objection* against this Hypothesis is, that it speaks of Souls as of *Faculties or* Powers, and not as of things that are Essentially *Active*; whereas a Soul is a *Knowledge*, a Cogitation; or at least a thing that is always Busie and Doing; insomuch, that even in sleep it does not all Rest, but that Men do always Dream when they sleep, tho' perhaps they are not always sensible, that they do.

I know not how truly it is said, that the Soul is always Busie, and that Men do always *Dream* when they sleep; but I could wish they did only Dream at that Time; for then we should not be Troubled with so many Groundless Fantastick Opinions. But to come nearer the Matter, I know a Person who Affirms, that, to his Knowledge, he *never* Dreamt in his whole Life; and certainly, since we are
always

always *Conscious* that we Dream, when ever we do, we ought to believe we have not Dreamed at all, when we are not sensible we have. Besides, *how* do they know that the Soul is always Doing? for my part, I am much mistaken if I do not Experience in my self (what I think any other may) that I am able to *suspend* all Thought, or (as we commonly Express it) think of nothing. To be sure, every one who hath made the Least Reflexion must needs know, that as we have Eyes, and Ears, and other sensitive Organs, and so do see, and hear, and are Conscious of other Sentiments, in Case our Eyes and Ears and those other Organs which we have, are Impressed by External Objects; so (ordinarily) we do neither see, nor Hear, or are Conscious of any other sentiment of any External *Objects*, if *these* do not Affect our Organs: without the presence of Objects we are only said to have the *Faculties* or Powers, that is, we are said, only to be *Able* to see, to Hear, *&c.* but upon the presence of Objects, and the Application of our Faculties or Powers, we are said to have the *Exercise* of them, and actually to See and Hear, *&c.* Thus it is in the External *Sense*. Now, since the *Mind* or Understanding is an Organical thing as well as the External sense, I

see

see no Reason to think, but that as there is no Actual Sensation but when the Organs of the sense are stirred, so there is no Actual Intellection but when that of the Understanding is; and that tho' we have always the Power of Understanding, as we have that of seeing, yet we do not actually Exercise that Power, but when it is *drawn into Act*, by some Impression upon it, either from the *Will* within, or from *Objects* without; any more than we do Actually see, *&c.* but when the Eye, *&c.* is Affected. In fine, since nothing of Cogitation is done within us by the Soul *Immediately*, but only by *means* of the Understanding, or of the will, or of the sense, External, or Internal, and All these are rather Faculties than Actions, I believe I have Reason to Conclude, that the Soul is rather a System of the Faculties, or else a Principle of them, than that it is a Perpetual never ceasing Exercise or Action, It is rather *Actus*, than *Actio*, in the Language of the Schools. And tho' in the Opinion of these, it be Essentially an Act, *Actus Corporis*, an Informing *form* to the Body, yet, in other Respects it is but *Actus Primus*, not *Actus Secundus*; for tho' it be an Original Principle of Action, and so an Active Power, yet, in it self, it is but a Power, and not Actually Active, or

Acting

Acting, but in the Requisite Circumstances. Thus we are Obliged to speak, to wit, *inadequately*, in the Notions of *Power* and *Act*, or Faculties and Exercise. And thus much for the First Objection.

The *Second* is, that in this *Hypothesis*, in the last Result, God is made the *Immanent* cause, whereas Really, and according to the truth of Revelation, Gen. 1. he is only a *Transient* Cause of all things. But to this the *Answer* is Easie; for tho' in Gen. 1: God is Represented (as he is in Reality) to be the Almighty Creator of all, and so as a Transient Cause, yet in this sense, he is also the *Immanent*, that, by the Mosaical Spirit, he giveth Life and Being, and Motion unto all; and this according to the *Apostle*, who says, that *in him* we live, and move, and have our being; as well as to Common *Metaphysicks*, which tell us, that all Beings are either First, or second Beings; and that Second Beings are *Participations* of the First. And however strange it may Look now, it was certainly of Old, the Common sentiment of all the Wiser part of the World; the *Jewish* Doctors, as well as Gentile *Philosophers*, and even of many *Ancient Fathers* of the Christian Church; it would be Superfluous, as well as Tedious, to mention all (if I could,) and therefore to

confine

confine my self within Fitting Bounds, I will instance two or three of the Chief for Examples. The first shall be *Apuleius* in his Book *de Mundo* (a Book ascribed to *Aristotle*, and by *Huetius* to *Posidonius*, and for certain it was originally *Greek*,) where he says, *vetus opinio est, atque Cogitationes omnium hominum penitus Insedit, Deum Essentiæ originis haberi Auctorem, Deumque ipsum salutem esse & Perseverantiam earum quas effecerit rerum, neque ulla Res est quæ viduata dei Auxilio, sui naturâ contenta sit. HancOpinionem vates secuti profiteri ausi sunt, omnia Jove plena esse.* It is an Ancient Opinion, and imprinted on the hearts of all Mortals, *&c.* And afterwards he adds, *Sed cum credamus Deum per omnia permeare, & ad nos, & ad ultra, potestatem sui nominis tendere, quantum abest, vel Imminet, tantum Existimandum est eum amplius minusve rebus utilitatis dare.*

Tho' it is true, that in conclusion he compares God to a Great King, that does many things by his Ministers.

The second shall be *Seneca*, who in his 6<th Epistle, among many other expressions to the same purpose, has this in so many words. *Quem in hoc Mundo Locum Deus Obtinet, hunc in homine Animus.* What God is, in reference to the World; that same the Soul is, in respect of a Man.

S

The third shall be the Emperor *Marcus Antoninus*, who in his *4th* Book, *Sect.* 40 τῶν εἰς ἑαυτὸν, says, ὡς ἓν ζῶον τὸν κόσμον, μίαν ουσίαν, κ̀ ψυχὴν μίαν ἐπέχον, συνεχῶς ἐπινοεῖν, &c. Be always minding that this World is like an Animal, that hath but one Substance or one Soul. I had not cited this Emperor, after I had cited *Seneca*, seeing both were *Stoicks*, but that in doing so I knew I should have occasion to refer my Reader to Mr. *Gataker*, who, in his Annotations on this passage of *Antoninus*, has made a large Collection of Authorities to the same intendment, which saves me a farther Labour.

The last that I will mention shall be a most Celebrated Father in the Christian Church, the great St. *Austin*, (for I omit the Excellent *Origen*, tho' as Learned as he, for being more obnoxious,) and I will cite the Testimony he gives, as I find it in a Schoolman, to show, that some even of the Schoolmen were in the same Opinion. *Orbellis* then (for he is the Schoolman I intend) upon the first of the Sentences, *Dist.* 8. *Q.* 2. says (just as *Seneca*) *Sicut Deus in Majori Mundo, sic Anima in Minori*; as God is in the greater World, so is the Soul in the lesser: and then by a simple Conversion of the Sentences, what the Soul is in the lesser World (of Man,) that

that God muſt be in the greater; and this he ſays is according to St. *Auguſtine, ſicut enim* (ſays he) *Deus eſt in Majori Mundo, ſic Anima in Minori, viz. in homine, ſecundum Auguſtinum.*

Only here it muſt be obſerved, that when *God* is compared unto a *Soul*, it muſt be underſtood with due limitation; to wit, as a Soul is taken only for a *Principle* of Powers and Actions, and not as it is an informing *Form*, or part of the Animal; for that God ſhould be a Soul in this latter ſenſe, is a notion no ways agreeing to him, who, in himſelf is all, and only perfection.

Another *Objection* is, that *God* and *Nature* are confounded in this Hypotheſis, ſo that it is not eaſie to ſay what is the intereſt of *God* in things, and what is *Natures*, or how they differ; to which I *Reply*, that indeed in the Holy Scriptures all is aſcribed to God, and the Spirit of God, without any mention of Nature; and yet ſince there are ſecond Cauſes, as well as a firſt, and ſo there is a thing which we call *Nature*, (for by this I now mean nothing but *ſecond Cauſes* and their working;) it will be very convenient to ſhow *how* God, how Nature does operate, and how they differ: and *this* perhaps may be done upon the propoſed *Hypotheſis* better than on any other.

other. For in *this*, God and Nature are distinguished, as the Soul of an Animal, and the System of Faculties; taking the Soul (as it is in the common Opinion) for the Principle of Faculties, and Faculties for the immediate Principles of all actions of Animals; and thus *Active Nature* is the System of all the Powers, all the Faculties of the Universe, and *God* the essential Principle of them. Or more plainly, since Faculties and Principles are notions rather than things, and some will be apt enough, without considering their grounds, to regard them only as meer notions, I shall therefore set out the difference that is between them, in more Real Expressions, by saying, that the *Influence* of God, or his active presence in things by means of the Mosaical Spirit, is as *Light*, and that *Nature*, (the System of all the Powers in the Universe) is as a Complex of all *Colours*; so that as Colour is the Modification of Light, and Light the essence of Colour, so particular Powers and Actions (that are but Powers in act,) are Modifications of the Divine Energy, and the Divine Energy the substance both of the Act and the Power; and thus the influence of the *first* and *second* Causes differ, as *Motion*, and *Modification* of Motion; the Motion arises from the *first*, the Modification from the *second* Cause,

Cause, either as it is an *Organ*, or as an *Object*: and so too, the *Aberrations* of Nature in Monsters, and in other instances, are accounted for, either by the ill Texture of the Organs, the over-whelming of matter, or by some other vitiosity and defect in the second Causes, without any impeachment of the first. As the scriblings of a bad mishaping Pen, are not imputed to the hand that guides it, which perhaps may be skilful enough) but to the Instrument that depraves the motion; and this, tho' the Motion comes from the Writer. In fine, I do not see any reason why *vital* Energy may not be *Imparted* and Communicated, as well as *Local*, which our sense evinces to be so: one Body that is in motion, striking another that is not, thereby *Communicates* its Motion to it; and *thus* a Cogitative vital *Energy* may *come* from God, and being *diffused* as Light is throughout the Universe, may be catched by agreeable Organs, and *Modified* by Objects, in the way that I have shewed before. I only hint this by way of Anticipation, to such as will inquire, whether this Cogitative vital Energy, diffus'd throughout the World, be *God* himself or no, or what it is; for there I stick, and call in the assistance and united force of greater understandings, mine beginning to be dazled with the lustre, or the subtilty of the Object: as yet I take it to be the *Mosaical Spirit*. So much for this *Objection*.

The *last* I shall propose is the Herculean one, that is insisted upon by many Great and very Judicious Men, which is, that if there is *but one* Original Perceptive throughout the Universe, all Animals would have the *same* Perceptions, so that what is known by *one*, could be ignored by *none*; ay, the same sentiments, the same Resentments, the same Pains, the same pleasures, that are in *any* one, would be in *every* one; and there could be no *Numerication*, no individuation of Spirits, or Souls, because *no separate*, particular Perceptions.

But this Objection as it is greater in appearance than in reality, so it can have little effect, if we consider, that it does equally destroy the *diversity* of Perceptions in the several Organs and Parts of *one* Animal, which yet our own Experience attests unto, as *that* of the perceptions of *several* Animals in the Universe; since, as there is but one Original Perceptive throughout the Universe, in the proposed Opinion; so in the common, there is but one in every Animal; and yet, tho' the *Soul* is but *one*, the *Faculties* are *many*, and the *exercises* of them *several*. For if but

one

one Eye is inflamed, the sense of Pain is *not* in *both*; and when but one Arm, or one Hand is wounded, the smart thereof is *only* in one; ay, the pains and ailments of the *Superior* Parts, are not felt in the *Inferior*, nor the sufferances of *these* in *those*; so that though the Animal it self may be said to have the Perception of all those of its several parts, yet these cannot be truly said to have one anothers. I acknowledge, that as the Soul may be said to have a common sense of all perceptions, but the several Members, each to have but a private sense for it self; so answerably, tho' the *Original Perceptive* is sensible of *all*, (and needs must, for he that made the Eye must needs see, and he that planted the Ear, must needs hear; and he that gave an heart unto man must needs understand,) yet *Particular Percipients*, particular Animals, as so many particular Organs must have *but* their share: one Animal can no more pretend to have the perceptions of another, (tho' the Original perceptive is the same in both, and is conscious to the perceptions of both) than in the same Animal the *Eye* can pretend to *Hear*, or the *Ear* to *See*, or either of them to *Smell*.

Hence it is evident, that the *Individuation* and Numerication of *Perceptions*, and consequently of Perceptive *Powers*, arises from the *Bodies*, or Organs, by means of which such perceptions are made; for where the *Bodies* are *separated*, or the Organs *distinct*, there the *Perceptions* made in those Bodies, and by means of such Organs are likewise *so*. In short, as I hinted before, perceptions and perceptive powers are individuated by *Bodies*, in the same ways as *Images* are by *Looking-Glasses*, or *Eccho's* by the contrivance of *Objects*.

But to demonstrate it in *Experience*, as well as by discourse, I will add a History or two of Monsters, that will do it plainly. The first shall be out of *Trivet*, and in his own Terms, (as I read them in an Ancient Manuscript) who reports the Accident just as *Sigebert* also does in his Chronicle add, *An.* 396. 'In the time of this *Valentinian*
'says he (but it should be as others say,
'in the time of *Theodosius*) at the Town of
'*Emaus* in *Jewry*, there was a *Child* bore,
'the which from the Navel upward, had
'*double* Body, that is to say double Breast,
'and double Head, and *proper* feeling of
'all parts; and sometimes the *one* sleepeth,
'and eateth, and drinketh, when the o-
'ther *doth* nought, and otherwise they
'eat, and drink, and sleep *together*; and
'sometimes they *weep* and *smile* together,
'and sometimes *strived* and chid together,
'and

'and when they were almoſt of two year
' Age, the one of them died four days be-
' fore the other.

Schenckius the Son, Reports another,
but reſembling ſtory, and with more Par-
ticularity and Circumſtance, and Conſequently more to our purpoſe, out of *Buchanan* his Scottiſh Hiſtory; *Monſtrum novi
generis* (ſays he) *in Scotiá natum eſt, infe-
riore quidem corporis parte ſpecie Maris, nec
quicquam à communi hominum formâ diſcre-
pans, Umbilicum vero ſupra, trunco corporis
ac reliquis omnibus membris geminis & ad
uſum atque ſpeciem diſcretis; id Rex dili-
genter & Educandum, & erudiendum curavit,
ac maxime in muſicis, quâ in re mirabiliter
profecit, quin & varias Linguas edidicit, &
variis voluntatibus duo Corpora ſecum diſcor-
diâ diſſentiebant, ac interim Litigabant, cum
aliud alii placeret, interim veluti in communi
conſultabant. Illud etiam in eo memorabile
fuit, quod cum inferna crura lumbive offende-
rentur, commune Corpus utrumque dolorem
ſentiret, cum vero ſuperne Pungeretur, aut
alioqui Læderetur, ad Alterum corpus tantum doloris ſenſus perveniret. Quod diſcri-
men in morte fuit magis Conſpicuum. Nam
cum alternum corpus complures ante alterum
dies extinctum fuiſſet, quod ſuperſtes fuit,
dimidio ſui Computreſcente paulatim contabuit.
Vixit id monſtrum Annos Viginti Octo, ac de-
ceſſit,*

cessit, Administrante rem Scoticam Joanne Prorege. Hac de re scribimus eo Confidentius, quod adhuc supersint homines honesti Complures, qui hæc viderint. So *Buchanan*, and *Schenkius* from him.

I will not give my self the trouble to translate the Relation, because I find it in Mr. *Ross* his continuation of Sir *Walter Rawleigh*'s History of the World, who thus tells the Story, *ad An.* 1490. About this time (says he) a strange Monster was born in *Scotland*, which *beneath* the Navel was *one* Body, but *above*, *two* distinct Bodies, having *different Senses*, Souls, and Wills; any hurt *beneath* the Navel is equally felt by *Both* Bodies above, but if any of the *upper* Members were hurt, *one* of the Bodies *only* felt the pain. This Monster the King caused to be instructed in Musick, and divers Languages. One of the Bodies died some days before the other, which also shortly after pined and consumed away. It lived Eight and Twenty years.

I might instance in many other Stories of this kind, but these suffice to evince what I induce them for, that the *numeration* of Souls, and consequently of other Spirits, depends upon *that* of Bodies; for in the alledged Examples, especially the latter, it is plain, that where the *Bodies*
were

were *divided* and separated, the *Powers* of Perception *likewise were*; so that the offences of but one, were not felt by both, but by one only; and yet again, in the parts beneath the Navel, common unto both the Bodies, any hurts in these were equally perceived by both. I take the *Theodosian* and *Scottish* Monsters to be evident illustrations of my Hypothesis. And so much for Substance, Harmonically considered.

CHAP.

CHAP. IX.

Of Substance in the Scholastical Consideration of it. Substance what, that it is First or Second. Second Substance is called a singular, a suppositum, or a subsistent. Of the Principle of Individuation, or that which makes a singular to be so. Dr. Sherlock's *Notion of the Individuation of Spirits. Of a Person. The true Idea of it.* Laurentius Valla *his notion of a Person, the unusefulness of it to the salving of the Holy Trinity shewed. The Trinity a Mystery, and Doctrine of Faith; not a Point of Philosophy; and so the Idea of it to be derived only from Revelation in the Holy Scriptures, and not from bare Discourses of Reason.*

I Have Discoursed of *Substance* after the *Harmonical* way, in the Precedent Chapters. It now remaineth that I add something concerning it in the *Scholastical*; and thus, Substance is defined to be a thing that is by it self, or that is under others called Accidents; and is divided into *First*, and *Second*. The Second Substance is that which is not in a Subject, but may be Prædicated of it, and such are Generical and Specifical Substances; as
for

for example, Living Creature, and Man; neither of which is in a subject, as an Accident is, but both are Prædicated of it; for Living Creature is Prædicated of *Man*, and Man of *Peter, James, John*, &c.

As for first Substance (which is the substance I design to speak of more particularly,) it is defined to be that which neither is in a Subject (as an Accident is,) nor is Prædicated of it, as the second substance is; it is also called a *Suppositum*, a subsistent, or a singular, in which is wont to be distinguished *Nature* and *Subsistence*; *Subsistence* is a mode of Existence, to which it adds Perseity, and *Existence* is Essence in Act; the *Nature* is the Idea or Definitive Conception of a Substance. Or thus, the *Nature* is the Thing or Substance as it is defined; a *Suppositum*, is the Thing or Substance that hath that Nature or Definition. Nature and Subsistence differ but as Essence and Existence; Subsistence being but the Existence of a substantial Nature. But Nature and a Suppositum Differ, as *Essentia* and *Ens*, the Former signifying (as the Schools speak) *ut Quâ*, the latter *ut Quod*.

In a singular Substance or *Suppositum*, that which comes particularly into Consideration, is the *Principle* (as Schollars call it) of *Individuation*, or that which makes a singular to become a singular, for the *Nature* is supposed to belong to one particular no more than to another, but to be a thing abstracted from all Particulars, and thence the question arises, what that is that *singularizes* the Nature; (for example, that of Man,) and makes it to belong to *Peter*, or to *John*, or to *James* in particular. This Principle of Individuation, (be it what it will,) may (as is thought by some,) be called the individuating *difference*; as well as that which does divide the *Genius* and constitute the Species, is called the specifical, since this individuating Principle doth as much divide the *Species*, and constitute the individual, as the specifical difference divides the *Genius*, and constitutes the species. Much ado there is what this Principle should be; but after all, they seem to me to come nearest to the Truth, who do affirm, that a singular or individual becomes so, not by any distinct Principle of individuation, but immediately and *per se*, and in that, that it is in being; just as *Quantity* is *Terminated* by self, and not by mediation of another Thing, that should confine and bound it; and in like manner is *Figured*, not by any thing superadded to it, but barely in that it is thus and thus Terminated.

I am

I am already almoſt tired with this idle fruitleſs way of talking, and ſhould not overcome my ſelf to proceed any farther in it, but that the *Notion* a Learned Perſon has of late delivered to the World, about the *Individuation of Spirits*, will oblige me to Conſider *it*, and by affording matter of more intelligible Diſcourſe, make ſome amends for the dryneſs and barrenneſs of the former. It is Dr. *Sherlock* I mean, who in his vindication of the Trinity, *S.* 4. *p.* 48. tells us, ' that in Created
' *Finite Spirits* their numerical oneneſs can
' be nothing but every Spirits *Unity*,
' within it ſelf, and diſtinct and ſeparate
' ſubſiſtence from all other Created Spirits;
' now this ſelf-unity of the Spirit can be
' nothing elſe but *ſelf-Conſciouſneſs*; that it
' is Conſcious to its own *Thoughts*, Reaſo-
' nings, Paſſions, which no other Spirit is
' Conſcious to but it ſelf. This makes a
' Finite Spirit *Numerically one*, and ſepa-
' rates it from all other Spirits, that every
' Spirit *feels* only its own *Thoughts* and *Paſ-*
' *ſions*, but is not Conſcious to the Thoughts
' and Paſſions of any other Spirit; and
' therefore if there were *three* Created Spi-
' rits ſo United as to be Conſcious each to
' others Thoughts, I cannot ſee any Rea-
' ſon why we might not ſay that three
' ſuch Perſons were *not* numerically one.
He

'He adds, let any Man, who can give me
'any other notion of the numerical One-
'ness of an *Infinite Mind* but self-consciouf-
'ness.

Thus this Learned Person.

It must be confessed, that the *Numerical Oneness* of Spirits can be nothing else but (as this Learned Author says it is) every Spirits *Unity* (he might as well have said Oneness) with it self, and its distinct and separate subsistence from all other Created Spirits. But this is not the oneness of *Spirits* only, but of *every* thing else that is one; for as *omne ens est unum*, so *unum est, quod est indivisum in se, & Divisum a quolibet Alio*; and therefore it doth hold in *Bodies* as well as in Spirits, and perhaps in the Infinite first Being, as well as in all Created Finite Beings. But to confine my self, as this Learned Author does, to the *Numerical Oneness of Spirits*; I cannot say farther of it, as he has, that it can be nothing else but *self-Consciousness*, in the sense of the word as he unfolds it, I say as he *Unfolds* it; for else, taking self-consciousness for a Spirits self-being, so I take it the numerical oneness of a Spirit is nothing but its self-consciousness, for then the meaning is, that a Spirit (which is a Cogitative Being) **is** *it self*, and not any other thing; but taking Consciousness as he does,

does, for a Spirits Being *sensible* of its own *Actions* and Passions, so its numerical oneness cannot be its self-consciousness. For as a Being (and even a Cogitative Being as a Being) must be conceived to *be*, before it can be conceived to *Act*; so again, it must be conceived to act, that is to *Think*, to *Reason*, to *Love*, to *Hate*, (for these are the Actions he instances in) for some moment of Reason *before* it can be conceived to be *Conscious* of these its actings. Now for that *Moment* of Reason, in which a Spirit is conceived *in Being*, without being conceived to be acting, and in which it is conceived *Acting* before it becomes *Conscious* of its actings, in that precedent moment, (which speaks *order*, not *duration*,) it must be conceived to be *one with it self*, and numerically different from every thing besides; and therefore that it is *so*, cannot arise from self-consciousness, or its being conscious of its own actings. So that if there were (as in the Authors supposal) *three* created Spirits, that were as conscious to each others Thoughts and Passions, as each of them unto his own, there would yet be no reason, that we should say (as he says we must) that three such persons would be numerically one; for if they were, how could they be Three? since the number Three, is not the number One, and they

T cannot

cannot be Three in number, if they are but one in number; to be Three is to be more than One; to be but One is not to be more than one. All that could be said of them is, that upon that supposal they would be *intimate* with one another, but with numerical distinction; for still one of them would not be the other, and so they would remain Three Persons still, not one Person. Self-Unity is before Self-Consciousness, and may consist with Consciousness of others. *Again*, in Dr. *Sherlock*'s way of Discoursing, which is, that Three Persons so intimate to one another as he supposes, would become numerically one, I do not see but that instead of the *Three* Persons of the Blessed *Trinity*, (which doubtless he will own to be really as intimate to one another, as he supposes his Three Finite ones to be,) we shall have but *one* Person (in number.) *In fine*, if Persons by being so intimate to one another do become numerically one, I do not see but that, by this reasoning, God who is as conscious to all the Actions, Passions, and Thoughts, of all Finite Created Spirits, as these are to their own, and as the Doctors Imaginary Persons are to one anothers, he must be numerically one with them all. But perhaps the Doctor will tell me, that he affirms the Three Eternal Minds (for so he calls them) are numerically

cally one *God*, not one *Perſon*, [Three Perſons, one God;] but then it will be demanded of him, ſince Three are *thrice one*, what that is that makes each Perſon one in it ſelf, and diſtinguiſhes it from both the others? for it muſt be ſomething that is not *Common*, which ſelf-conſciouſneſs is, (in his ſenſe of the word,) all being as conſcious to one anothers Thoughts and Actings, as each unto its own: whereas, *that* which makes a thing numerically one, muſt be *Differencing* and Particular. Not to inſiſt, that to be an Eternal Mind is the true *Idea* or notion of God, and then if there be (as he owns there be) Three Eternal Minds (really diſtinct,) it will I confeſs, be no great difficulty to evince them Three Perſons, but I doubt it will, intelligibly to make it out, that theſe Three (Three Eternal Minds, really diſtinct from one another,) are not Three *Gods*, as well as Three Perſons. So that methinks the knot remains untied. For my own part, I believe as the Scriptures inſtruct me, that there is but *one God*, tho' *Three Perſons*; each of which is *God*; which I ſay only to prevent Miſtakes. But I reſolve to Diſcourſe more fully of *Unity* or Oneneſs, when I come to treat of the notions of *Whole* and *Part*.

As for the name [Perſon] it properly belongs to *Men*; we do not commonly apply

ply it to *Beasts*, or unto *Angels*, or other Spirits, but by Translation and Metaphor, when they do appear in the Figure or shape of Men. Nor is [Person] a name of *Nature*, taking nature in the sense of the Schoolmen; for Nature is *Common* unto all of the kind, but that only is *Personal* which is distinguishing and peculiar among those in the same kind. Thus, *Man* is a name of the *kind*; or specifical Nature, the Nature in common; *A* Man an expression of the Nature as *singularized*; but *Person* properly is the name of that which differences Men from one another. When we speak of the Person of a Man, we mean by it that Cumble of Accidents, External, Internal, of Body, of Mind, Adventitious and Extrinsical, Absolute or Relative, whereby he is distinguished, and known from others. Hence *Persona* in Latin, is πρόσωπον in *Greek*, and πρόσωπον signifies the Countenance or Face, in the first place; and from thence, a Person, in the second (place,) because the Countenance or Face is that by which we do chiefly distinguish Men. In conformity to this Idea or notion of Person, I understand *Levit.* 19. 15. *Thou shalt not favour the* Person *of the Poor, nor honour the* Person *of the Mighty*; the word for Person is πρόσωπον in the Septuagint Translation, and the meaning of the Text is plainly
This,

This, thou shalt not in giving Judgment have regard to the Poverty of the one, or to the Riches of another; for these concern the *Person*, not the *Cause*. In this sense also is God said to be Ἀπροσωπολέπτης no *Accepter of Mens Persons*, for that he in judgement respects not (as Men too often do) the foreign *Qualities* and Accidents that do distinguish them from one another, as, their wit, or their weakness; their comeliness, or their deformity; their riches, or their Poverty; their Grandeur or their Littleness of Figure in the World. But all is as one to him, when he enters into Judgement; for he judges uprightly, according to the *merits of the Cause*, without regard to the Person, save where the Consideration of the Person is of moment (as sometimes it is) in the merits of the Cause. But as *the* Person of a Man is that bundle of Qualities that do distinguish him from others; so *A* Person is a Man with those Qualities; that is, a Person is a *Distinguished* Man; and so the word comes to be taken, not only for the *Qualities* that do distinguish, but for the *Man* that is distinguished, by those qualities; in which sense the word is used, not only by the *Schoolmen*, who after *Boetius*, define a Person to be a rational subsistent, *Rationalis Naturæ Individua substantia*; but by the *Apostle*, when he

speaks

speaks, 2 Cor. 1. 11. *of Thanks being given by many* Persons *for him.*

By what I have said (and I have said the more for that the cause of late has had a fresh Rehearing) we may judge of the justice of *Laurentius Valla*, who in his Elegance, *l.* VI. *c.* 34. severely, (or rather insolently) reflects upon *Boetius* for asserting that a Person was not a Quality or in any other Predicament but that of Substance; he shows in many instances, that [Person] signifies *Quality*, and thence infers, that the same man may sustain a hundred Persons; [*Quo fit,* says he, *ut Assit mihi Multiplex Persona ac Diversa, sed una tantum substantia;*] and to give an Example, he fancies himself a *Hector*, and says [*ad Priamum sum Personâ Filii, ad Astianacta personâ Patris, ad Andromacham personâ Viri; ad Paridem personâ Fratris; ad Sarpedonem personâ Amici; ad Achillem personâ Inimici.*] In fine, making application of what he says unto the *Deity*, he thinks that he has carried the Prize, by demonstrating *how* God may be but *one Substance*, and yet be *Three Persons*; But 'tis in a way in which his *Hector* may be a *Hundred*, and God as *many*, and more. So that I had not believed it worth my while to mention this Opinion, but that an *Excellent Person* of our own has given it fresh reputation, by going the same way; for the Learned Author of the *Three Sermons concerning the Sacred Triny,* shews, as *Laurentius Valla* does, that the word [Person] was used of old to signifie the *State,* Quality, or Condition of a Man, as he stands related to other Men, either as a *King,* or a *Subject,* or as *Father,* or a *Son,* &c. Thus he observes the Latin Phrase is *Personam Imponere* when a Man is

put

put into Office or a Dignity Conferred upon him; *Induere personam*, when he takes upon him the Office; *Sustinere personam*, when one bears, or Executes an Office, &c. In short, he tells us, (as *Laurentius Valla* has) that 'tis nothing strange for the *same* man to sustain *Divers* Persons, instancing in *Tully*, who says; *Sustineo unus Tres Personas, Meam, Adversarii, Judicis*, I being but one, do yet sustain Three Persons, my own, that of an Adversary, and that of a Judge. *In fine*, he makes the same application of it to the Divine Trin-unity that *Laurentius Valla* doth, for (says he) if Three Persons may be one man, what hinders but that Three Divers Persons may be one God? and that the *same God* as Maker of the World, or God the Creator may be God the *Father*; and as Author of our Redemption be God the *Redeemer*, or God the *Son*; and as working effectually in the hearts of his Elect, be God the Sanctifier or God the *Holy Ghost*.

I confess if this is *all* that is in the Mystery, it is very Conceiveable, and (which will be an unvaluable happiness to the Christian World) there will need to be no more dispute about it: but as the *Received Doctrine* of the Divine Trin-unity is quite another thing, so must it have a very different *Exposition*. Besides, *Laurentius Valla* seems to suppose that the difficulty is only about the *word* [Person,] But this is his mistake; for the word [Person] as applied to the Trinity is but of a *later* use, and of the *Schoolmen*, rather than of the *Fathers*, whose word is *Hypostasis*, which is also the *Apostles* word: So that unless it can be found, that one Man can be three *Hypostases*, or Subsistents, and that for God to be a Creator, a Redeemer, and a Sanctifier, is,

to

to be three *Hypostases* in the *Fathers* sense, as well as Three *Persons* in *Cicero's*, the *Difficulty* is not removed, but only avoided. *In fine*, it is not the same thing to say that one *sustains* Three Persons, as to say that one *is* Three Persons: For he that only sustains a Person, doth but *Act* the part of that Person which he is said to sustain; and thus *Cicero* sustained Three Persons, when he acted as if he had been Three several Men under different Characters: To *Personate* a Judge is not *to be* one: And in this sense of the word Person *Seneca* says, *Ep.* 24. *non hominibus tantum, sed & Rebus PERSONA Demenda est, & reddenda facies sua.*

I say not this with any intention to enter into a Discourse of the Divine Trin-unity, the doing of which would be improper, in a Treatise that pretends but to Metaphysicks: I have only mention'd it on occasion, as an inquiry after the Idea and notion of a *Suppositum*, and that of a *Person*, obliged me. The *Doctrine* of the *Trinity* is a point of pure *Revelation*, not of *Philosophy* or Science; all Discourses and explications of it, not derived from the Holy Scriptures, and grounded upon them, but on Analogies and Resemblances in *nature*, or on Principles of Human *Discourse* and meer Reason, are as Foreign unto it, as Earth is to Heaven. It is an Article of Faith, and a Fundamental one too; indeed the chief of all those of which the *Apostle* says, they are such as *neither Eye saw, nor Ear heard of, nor entred into the heart of man to conceive,* before they were brought to light in the Gospel. Wherefore, 'tis there only that we are obliged to seek it, and there only, in the *Analogy* of Faith, that we can hope to discover it, in its true Idea and Notion. And so much for Substance as Scholastically Consider'd.

FINIS.